The Word of God is a lamp unto our feet and a light unto our paths (Psalm 119:105). To have the lamp is important, but to make it shine for illumination and direction is far more advantageous. Kwadwo O. Appiah-Kubi provides you with simple, but practical daily directions full of wisdom, instructions, encouragement and empowerment for successful living. **366 NUGGETS FROM SCRIPTURES** is **one-of-a-kind**; a brilliant piece of work.

Rt. Rev. Dr. Akwasi Asare Bediako
Bishop and General Overseer,
Resurrection Power &
Living Bread Ministries Int.

Jesus said, "I am the vine, you are the branches. He who abides in Me, and I in him, bears much fruit; for without Me you can do nothing" (John 15:5). This book, **366 NUGGETS FROM SCRIPTURES**, is **a master piece**. It will help you to remain in the LORD Jesus Christ; to grow and mature in your daily walk with Him. By reading and applying the principles of this book it will enable you to increase in faith so as to soar on the wings of eagles in this life.

Prophet Samuel Frimpong (M.Phil)
Senior Pastor, Higher Life Assemblies
of God, Tesano, Accra

Kwadwo through this year-round book brings to the fore God's profound statement, **man shall not live by bread alone but by every word that proceeds from the mouth of God**. The **TRUTH** in this book will greatly nourish your soul and make your life truly a fulfilled one. **Great work** indeed.

Rev. Dr. Boakye Acheampong
Regional Overseer, Resurrection Power
& Living Bread Ministries Int.,
Accra-East.

As the body obtains essential nutrients from daily food consumption, so does the spirit and the soul thrive on God's Word. Kwadwo has presented a simple but effective way of deriving spiritual nourishments from daily exposition of Scriptures. This book is important even for the non-Christian, how much more the believer? It will serve as daily medicine to your soul. This is **a must-read**.

Rev. Emmanuel K. Asamoah
Regional Overseer, Resurrection Power
& Living Bread Ministries Int., USA

366 NUGGETS FROM SCRIPTURES VOLUME I

A Brief, In-depth Exploration of Scriptures

KWADWO OSEI APPIAH-KUBI

authorHOUSE®

AuthorHouse™
1663 Liberty Drive
Bloomington, IN 47403
www.authorhouse.com
Phone: 1 (800) 839-8640

Published by AuthorHouse 01/22/2016

ISBN: 978-1-5049-7514-8 (sc)
ISBN: 978-1-5049-7515-5 (e)

This book is dedicated to:

My father, Osei Kwabena Asibey, of blessed memory. You will forever be missed.

The men of God, who have imparted grace and knowledge to my life.

Foreword

Reading a document becomes relevant and effective when it is well understood; so is the Bible. Some people, including non-Christians, find it difficult to accept the Bible because it does not make sense to them due to the lack of understanding. The Bible is the traveler's map, the pilgrim's staff, the pilot's compass, the soldier's sword, and the Christian's charter, and thus a necessity for life. It is the quest of every committed Christian to develop deeper understanding of the Scriptures. Reading the Bible can be a routine with little or no understanding which can be boring and frustrating.

366 NUGGETS FROM SCRIPTURES provides you the opportunity to acquaint yourself with several Scriptures. Kwadwo O. Appiah-Kubi brings to bare simple but profound explorations of Scriptures; with practical explanations that can be applied to daily experiences. He deals with topics including hope, faith, love, prayer, praise, thanksgiving, anxiety, obedience, service and success.

Each day has a Scripture that is expounded phrase by phrase, word by word, to bring out both spiritual and other related meanings in diversity. The Scripture is considered in the context of the whole passage in order to provide background information and import of the message. The author offers the platform to establish a daily relationship with the Word of God.

I have known Kwadwo for more than a decade. He has been a great influence to many, particularly to the youth ministry for many years, in organizing generational leaders through the Word of God, which has giving him a deepest understanding to bring these revelations to your heart in simple ways.

366 NUGGETS FROM SCRIPTURES will build up your Christian journey with a deeper understanding of the Word of God. It brings out the author's daily experiences with God's Word, and the knowledge, wisdom and understanding he has gained over the years with people and life situations. This book in your hand will be a guide to enable you experience a successful life on daily basis. It will be a daily tool which will enable you overcome all sorts of life challenges, and a weapon which will enable you to take absolute dominion of all that belongs to you as Child of God.

As you read and apply the principles of this book avail yourself to the Holy Spirit, the Author of the Scriptures, to usher you to new areas of enlightenment so you can have constant success.

Rev. Dr. Yaw Owusu Ansah
Regional Overseer,
Resurrection Power & Living
Bread Int., Accra West
(Adom Fm)

Shalom
God's Blessings
YOA

Preface

It is a joyful experience to get a deeper understanding of the Scriptures. It enables us to know the mind of God so we can apply His principles for effective living. Amazingly, when we read the same Scripture at different times God gives us new revelations, which signifies that His Word is always refreshing and relevant to every situation.

This book came to being as a result of my daily commitment to studying the Word of God. Nearly two decades ago, the LORD inspired me to document the revelations and ideas He gives me as I spend time in His Word. Little did I know that He was preparing the opportunity to share His mind to the benefits of others. Like every field of study, through the gaining of knowledge and revelations from the teachings of the Holy Spirit, I developed this manuscript. I call these knowledge and revelations NUGGETS because they are valuable life principles.

366 NUGGETS FROM SCRIPTURES comprises a daily exploration of several Scriptures from the Holy Bible all year round. It brings to you daily spiritual nourishments that will enable you to understand many Bible verses and to practically and effectively apply them in your daily life for consistent successes throughout the year. This edition contains 182 days, with seven to ten nuggets for each day; resulting into over 1,450 nuggets. Although some of the nuggets may seem repeated, this is purported to place emphasis and encourage memorization so you can effectively apply them. At the beginning of each week is a quote from people who have made great impact.

The purpose of the book is to provide insights into the knowledge, truth and revelations from the Bible. It gives a multidimensional perspective of the Scriptures; that is, a holistic view so that it can be applied to every facet of life. Remember, half-truth can be dangerous. Some Christians do not realize the effectiveness of the Scriptures because they do not consider the holistic view of a theme of interest. They read the Scriptures out of context and miss out the ability to combine all possible situations in order to achieve the full benefits. Others also do not explore other related Scriptures of the same theme of interest. The ability to reconcile two or more Scriptures that seem to be contrasting is the revelation God gives to those who are dedicated to search His mind.

366 NUGGETS FROM SCRIPTURES is not designed to give detailed explanations but succinct exploration of the Scriptures that is easy to read, meditate, memorize, recollect and apply to your daily life. Common Biblical words and terms are defined, explained in general terms and in context with regards to the specific verse. The book is written to teach, correct, equip and inspire you to live a well-fulfilled life through topics such as faith, love, prayer, thanksgiving and service. It will assist you to develop a closer relationship with God which will cascade to your relationships with others. This book will also give you the opportunity to document specific actions you would like to take in order to improve specific areas of your life and impact the life of others.

How to use this book effectively:

1. You can use it to gain further understanding of some selected verses from Scripture and/or as your daily devotional guide. In order to maximize the benefit of this book read the main scriptural passage first.
2. Meditate on the Scriptural verse and allow the Holy Spirit to give you insight.
3. Read through and reflect on the nuggets for further explanation. Write out new revelations the LORD shows to you.
4. Think about how you can translate the nuggets to specific areas of need in your life and take action immediately. Commit yourself to these actions by writing them down in the "What action(s) will I take today to improve my life?"
5. Pray and confess that God will enable you to put these actions into practice. The Prayer at the end of each day is not conclusive, but a model to engage you in an intensive, effective and fervent communication with God.
6. Reassess your actions at most on weekly basis to see how well your life is improving in that area until you gain mastery over it.
7. It is suggested that you commit reading **366 NUGGETS FROM SCRIPTURES** daily.

Acknowledgment

To Rt. Rev. Dr. Akwasi Asare Bediako, Rev. Dr. Boakye Acheampong, Rev. Dr. Yaw Owusu Ansah, Rev. Emmanuel K. Asamoah and Prophet Samuel Frimpong. Thank you for believing in me.

To Fredrick Agyiri and Sharms Donkor for taking time off their busy schedules to edit this book. Thank you for your great inputs.

To my lovely wife, Agnes Appiah-Kubi, who contributed immensely to these nuggets. Thank you for believing in and inspiring me to greater heights. You are indeed a woman of substance.

To my brother from another mother, Jacobus Patterson for his ideas, encouragement and support. Thank you for making this book a reality.

The key to power is the ability to judge who is best
able to further your interests in all situations

Robert Greene (48 Laws of Power)

January 1

Develop Self-control

Scripture reading: Proverbs 25:21-28

Proverbs 25:28
Whoever has no rule over his own spirit is like a city broken down, without walls.

1. Self-control is the ability of an individual to take charge of his own life in order to consistently do the right thing.
2. Self-control is the ability of an individual to prevent situations from causing him/her to react by impulse. This individual does not allow the environment or circumstance to determine/ influence how he/she constantly feels, thinks and particularly acts.
3. Self-control is the Christian's ability to allow the Holy Spirit to control his/her life. He/she does not act based on his/her own will/desire. In fact, he/she does not have a will but that of the Holy Spirit. Every Christian must crave for this spirit (i.e. self-control), which is one of the fruit of the Spirit.
4. Self-control is a defense. It prevents the environment and situations from determining your actions.
5. Lack of self-control can make one lose all that he/she has built over the years; reputation, respect, trust, wealth etc.
6. The devil can easily attack you by breaking down your self-control.
7. A city is noted for high standards of buildings, technologies and precious items of importance. An enemy can successfully attack and overcome a nation only when he conquers the city. So it is for the enemy to attack you if he gets access to your heart. Guard the walls to your heart.
8. Anger is the cousin of loss of self-control. Anger quickly emerges when you lose self-control.

Prayer: LORD Jesus, please enable me to develop the attitude of self-control in all my endeavors. Let me allow the Holy Spirit to continue to instill this fruit into me.

What action(s) will I take today to improve my life?

_____

_____

_____

_____

January 2

Benefits of Singing to the LORD

Scripture reading: Psalm 59:9-16

Psalm 59:16
But I will sing of Your power. Yes, I will sing aloud of Your mercy in the morning; For You have been my defense and refuge in the day of my trouble.

1. In times of trouble/danger reflect on the strength of God; reflect on the power of God to deliver you (instead of allowing fear to grip you).
2. Singing is a powerful weapon we need especially when we are downhearted. Singing hymns and praises to God evokes His presence and disperses the activities of Satan.
3. Sing about God's love at all times, in good and bad times.
4. God demonstrates His love towards us every morning. The fact that we wake up every morning is an evidence of His love towards us.
5. The more you sing about the attributes of God the more you see them manifest in your life. You attract what you constantly declare.
6. God is your defense. Always rely on Him for everything.
7. You can experience the refuge (protection) of God only if you abide in His fortress (castle); that is, abide in His Word.

Prayer: Lord Jesus, instill within me an attitude of singing and praising You at all times. In times of challenges help me obtain strength from You through singing.

What action(s) will I take today to improve my life?

_____
_____
_____
_____

Joy is the mother of all inspiration, because your spirit-man, the source of inspiration, is at its best when you are joyful. When you are depressed, your spirit-man is broken, but joy is the health of the spirit-man

Bishop David Oyedepo (Exploring the Secrets of Success)

January 3

God's Power to Forgive

Scripture reading: Psalm 103:1-12

Psalm 103:12
As far as the east is from the west, so far has He removed our transgressions from us.

1. Forgiveness is a powerful panacea God gave to us so we can constantly be in fellowship with Him.
2. Our role in this forgiveness provision is to genuinely request for it and God's role is to grant it.
3. When God forgives us He remembers it no more. It is as though we never sinned; we obtain the righteousness of God.
4. Learn to believe in God's forgiveness and forgive yourself also.
5. God's duty is to forgive you. It is your duty to forgive yourself; otherwise Satan will always torment you with guilt (which in itself is sin).
6. Although the forgiveness of God is ever present, we should not abuse it (Romans 6:1). For we do not know when we may not get the chance to confess our "habitual sin". Death can take you anytime.
7. When we continue to sin (because we think God is forgiving), it may reach a time that we may not have the conviction (from the Holy Spirit) to confess anymore. We then begin to see sin as a normal part of life and the devil begins to possess our heart.

Prayer: Heavenly Father, I thank you for Your provision of forgiveness. Help me to accept Your forgiveness so that the enemy will not cause me to live in guilt. In Jesus' Name.

What action(s) will I take today to improve my life?

_____

_____

_____

_____

January 4

Serving from the Heart

Scripture reading: Deuteronomy 11:1-15

Deuteronomy 11:13
And it shall be that if you earnestly obey My commandments which I command you today, to love the Lord your God and serve Him with all your heart and with all your soul.

1. God requires faithfulness from us in all that we do.
2. Some Christians obey part of God's Word that suits or appeals to them, but ignore the unappealing parts.
3. God's commands/Word should not be partially observed, but it should be obeyed fully and faithfully.
4. Anytime you read/hear God's command in the Bible realize that it is for you; that day God is speaking to you.
5. We can remain faithful to God by loving Him in all situations.
6. When love precedes in our relationship with God, faithfulness becomes spontaneous.
7. Love the Lord and serve Him with all your heart and with all your soul.
8. Service to God must emanate from a loving heart, else it is hypocrisy and no reward should be expected.
9. When we commit our entire heart and mind to God nothing else can control us.

Prayer: Dear God, please help me to love You with all my heart and all my soul, so I will always obey you from a genuine heart.

What action(s) will I take today to improve my life?

_____

_____

_____

_____

January 5

Daily Bread from God

Scripture reading: Luke 11:1-4

Luke 11:3
Give us day by day our daily bread.

1. God has given us the opportunity to ask anything we desire according to His will and He will do it.
2. As a child of God it is your right to ask for your desires from your heavenly Father.
3. God is a great provider but until you ask He will not fulfill your desires.
4. Asking something from God is not wishing; it is praying to Him- having a personal relationship with Him.
5. Every day has its own needs, ask God for His provision.
6. The "bread" in this verse is referring to God's Word– Jesus Christ. It is God's Word that has the divine creative ability to produce anything we need; to give us all our provisions.
7. God has a specific Word for you every day. You may not realize this until you have your quiet time (bible devotion) every day.
8. You need to ask God for your daily bread (i.e. His Word) to make your life successful.
9. God's will can be done in your life only when you ask for His specific Word concerning that matter.
10. It is God's joy that He provides for us when we ask Him by faith.

Prayer: Heavenly Father, let me understand the power of your Word. Let me know that I need Your Word every day to go through life victoriously.

What action(s) will I take today to improve my life?

_____
_____
_____
_____

January 6

Put your Hope in God

Scripture reading: Lamentations 3:22-26

Lamentations 3:25
The Lord is good to those who wait for Him, to the soul who seeks Him.

1. God is a principled God and therefore upholds His Word/Laws. He is committed to His Word.
2. When you go according to His Word you will enjoy His goodness. When you do otherwise you will face His wrath (i.e. the consequences).
3. When you put your hope in the LORD you will obtain His goodness.
4. The goodness of God is an evidence of His glory upon our lives.
5. When we trust in the LORD, we see His goodness, which in turn makes us trust Him more and the cycle grows.
6. Those whose hope is in God are those who believe in Him and obey His Word.
7. Constantly seeking God builds up your relationship with Him. It makes it easier to abide in His Word and enjoy His goodness.
8. When your hope is in God you do not fear what the enemy tries to do against you.

Prayer: LORD Jesus, despite the challenges of life please teach me to put my hope in You at all times. Help me to solely depend on Your Word so that I can continue to enjoy Your goodness.

What action(s) will I take today to improve my life?

_____

_____

_____

_____

January 7

Antidotes for Anxiety

Scripture reading: Philippians 4:1-7

Philippians 4:6
Be anxious for nothing, but in everything by prayer and supplication, with thanksgiving, let your requests be made known to God.

1. Anxiety is unhealthy to the soul, spirit and body.
2. When you are constantly anxious in life check your level of faith and maturity in Christ.
3. Anxiety may come naturally but how you handle it is the issue.
4. Those whose hope and faith are in God overcome anxiety.
5. When you allow God to nurture and build up your faith things that used to make you anxious will later become nothing.
6. Replace all your anxieties with prayers; trust in God's Word; thanksgiving; and a cheerful heart.
7. Instead of complaining about the situation present it to God in prayer.
8. Many spend more time complaining about the situation and little or no time in chatting (praying) with God about the same situation.

Prayer: LORD enable me to understand that I should not be anxious when any difficult situation happens in my life. Teach me to trust in You at all times because You are the All-knowing God.

What action(s) will I take today to improve my life?

_____
_____
_____
_____

January 8

The Purpose of God's Deliverance

Scripture reading: Deuteronomy 15:1-15

Deuteronomy 15:15
You shall remember that you were a slave in the land of Egypt, and the Lord your God redeemed you; therefore I command you this thing today.

1. Always remember the low places God has taken you from. It will help keep you humble and enable you to continually depend on Him.
2. Always remember the goodness of the Lord in your life. It will help you to continually trust Him and have an expectant and promising future.
3. Never attribute your progress in life to your own strength or wisdom, but to the Lord.
4. When we recognize the goodness of God it helps us to easily obey His commands for our lives; we attribute our existence (life) to Him and acknowledge that we depend solely on Him.
5. If God was able to save you by the blood of His only Begotten Son (Jesus Christ), then He is well able to deliver you from every situation and meet all your needs.
6. When you face difficult situations in life, remember that the same God who once brought you from a previous one is well able to deliver you.
7. God has set you free from the bondage of sin and Satan, so you can also avail yourself to be used by God to set others free.

Prayer: Dear LORD, please give me the understanding to remember where You took me from so I will always fulfill the purpose of Your deliverance in helping others.

What action(s) will I take today to improve my life?

_____

_____

_____

_____

January 9

The Heart of a Child

Scripture reading: Matthew 18:1-6

Matthew 18:3
And [Jesus] said, "Assuredly, I say to you, unless you are converted and become as little children, you will by no means enter the kingdom of heaven.

1. Asking intelligent questions elicit great answers and lessons; it brings a lot of revelations.
2. The Word of God is always true. Just accept that and your life will be better and better day by day.
3. To attain a particular feat, change is necessitated. Without change nothing can change. Without change everything will definitely remain the same.
4. Change therefore starts from the mind. Until you change your thought processes your attitude will not change.
5. If you do not allow God's Word and His Spirit to change your mind it will be impossible to please Him
6. You can become a better Christian by changing from the wrong and bad attitudes into what the Word of God has commanded you to do.
7. When it comes to obeying God's Word, let us become like little children who know nothing except what their father tells them. They know not any other truth or principle except the one given by their father.
8. When we become like little children we will have a humble heart/spirit to readily obey God's Word than thinking we have arrived and therefore want to live by our own principles.
9. Pride and a haughty spirit can cause you to refuse God's Word and unfortunately miss heaven.

Prayer: I am grateful LORD for giving me the grace to adopt the heart of a child. Please help me to believe Your Word regardless of the situations surrounding me.

What action(s) will I take today to improve my life?

_____

_____

_____

_____

Faith is not in the realm of the five physical senses, since it is the proof of things we do not see and perceive by our senses. It's a spiritual force, an attribute of the human spirit

Pastor Chris Oyakhilome (How to Make Your Faith Work)

January 10

Pure Grace

Scripture reading: 2 Thessalonians 1:1-4

2 Thessalonians 1:2
Grace to you and peace from God our Father and the Lord Jesus Christ.

1. Grace is the product of Jesus Christ dying for the redemption of our sin so that we can have a relationship with God.
2. Grace therefore is Jesus Christ.
3. Grace is the ability God has given us to become His children.
4. Grace is the ability God has given us to do things that we naturally are incapable of.
5. Peace is enjoying the goodness of God, whether in good or bad times.
6. Peace is not the absence of war or troubles.
7. Peace is experiencing calmness and inner stillness in the midst of trouble.
8. You may not appreciate the peace of God unless tough times come.
9. True peace is established when we learn to trust God in all circumstances and solely depend on Him.

Prayer: Thank You Jesus for giving me Your perfect grace. Your grace indeed has brought me peace. Use me to share Your grace with others so they can also enjoy Your peace.

What action(s) will I take today to improve my life?

_____
_____
_____
_____

January 11

A Sacrifice to God

Scripture reading: Romans 1:1-8

Romans 12:1
I beseech you therefore, brethren, by the mercies of God, that you present your bodies a living sacrifice, holy, acceptable to God, which is your reasonable service.

1. Sometimes you need to softly instruct people in order to get their attention to follow your instruction (advice). To attract people's attention, show care and concern for their welfare and find ways to identify with and to connect with them.
2. Although Christ has saved us from sin, He's still given us our will. It is left to us to offer/sacrifice our bodies to God.
3. If we do not fully offer our bodies to God, Satan will still be controlling us through the desires of our bodies and our relationship with God will fall short and be ineffective.
4. I perceive that "body" used here by Apostle Paul to be the soul and not the physical, biological body. This is because the soul usually influences the body.
5. You offer your body to God by sacrificing (i.e. giving up) your will, mind (intellect) and emotions to Him. You no longer follow your desires but that of Christ.
6. When you put your will, mind and emotions, (all of which constitute your soul), under the control of the Holy Spirit you automatically sacrifice your body to God.
7. Until you have sacrificed your body to God, any other sacrifice you present to Him is not alive (living).
8. A body sacrificed to God is a living sacrifice. That is, you are living for God, and not for yourself.
9. When you sacrifice your whole body to God it becomes holy and pleasing to Him.

Prayer: Heavenly Father, let me sacrifice my whole being to You, so I can please You at all times.

What action(s) will I take today to improve my life?

_____

_____

_____

_____

January 12

Living for Christ

Scripture reading: Romans 6:1-14

Romans 6:13
And do not present your members as instruments of unrighteousness to sin, but present yourselves to God as being alive from the dead, and your members as instruments of righteousness to God.

1. As a Christian, although you have given your life to God, He has given your will to you.
2. Unless you totally handover your will to God you are still the master of your life. That is, salvation does not mean automatic control by God; you need to submit your entire will to Him before He takes control.
3. After salvation God gives you the power over sin. It is your own will to decide whether or not to continue sinning; this is not God's responsibility.
4. If a Christian keeps on sinning, then it means he hasn't fully committed that aspect of his life to Christ.
5. Do not allow yourself to become instruments/tools of sin/wickedness.
6. Allow yourself to be used by God as tools of righteousness.
7. Never forget that you were bought (at a price) from death into life. If you always remember this grace, you will place a great value on yourself and realize you need to live above sin. You will realize that you are not cheap to be yo-yoed by Satan. You are a royal priesthood, a holy nation, and one chosen by God. You will also realize that God owns you; you do not own your life.

Prayer: I receive Your strength to live above sin so I will not offer my body as instruments of unrighteousness, in Jesus' Name. Amen.

What action(s) will I take today to improve my life?

_____

_____

_____

_____

January 13

Strength of the Youth

Scripture reading: 1 John 2:7-14

1 John 2:14b
I have written to you, young men, because you are strong, and the word of God abides in you, and you have overcome the wicked one.

1. God has given strength as a special gift to young men and women. We should therefore value and appreciate it and use it effectively to His glory.
2. As a young person, your greatest asset is the Word of God because He becomes the solid foundation of your life. You live your life according to this foundation and success is guaranteed if you remain faithful to God's Word.
3. The strength of God can be perfected in our lives if we allow His Word to live richly in us.
4. The Word of God dwells richly in those who live by the Word (or work with the Word), but not those who have merely committed it to memory.
5. The Word of God is Jesus Christ Himself. If we allow Him to lead our lives we will experience success in every facet of our lives.
6. It is only the Word of God in you that will give you strength to overcome the evil one.
7. There are many battles in the lives of young people. You need the Word of God to strengthen you in order to win the battles.

Prayer: Dear LORD enable me to receive strength from You by living according to Your Word.

What action(s) will I take today to improve my life?

_____
_____
_____
_____

January 14

True Love is Unconditional

Scripture reading: Luke 6:27-36

Luke 6:32
But if you love those who love you, what credit is that to you? For even sinners love those who love them.

1. Everyone, good or evil, exhibit some kind of love or the other. Ordinarily, when love is expressed, people tend to reciprocate. Loving a fellow lover is therefore not a big deal.
2. If you love those who love you, it is more of a conditional love. Your love becomes authentic when such people wrong you and you still love them.
3. Love should be exhibited with no expectation of reward. It should be unconditional; otherwise your reward will come from the recipient (man) instead of God.
4. Love unconditionally, expecting your reward from God (not from man).
5. Your true worth as a Christian is realized by the world when you exhibit unconditional, selfless love.
6. The highest level of love is to love those who hate you (i.e. the unlovable) or those who irritate you.
7. When you make loving people a lifestyle, (through the help of the Spirit of God) you don't struggle to exhibit it irrespective of the recipient, the location or the time.

Prayer: God, please train my heart to love people unconditionally, even including my enemies.

What action(s) will I take today to improve my life?

_____
_____
_____
_____

January 15

Revive a Disturbed Soul

Scripture reading: Psalm 42:1-11

Psalm 42:11
Why are you cast down, O my soul? And why are you disquieted within me?
Hope in God; for I shall yet praise Him, the help of my countenance and my God.

1. It is normal to have a disturbed/troubled/worried soul when circumstances are tough. However, what matters is the way you handle it.
2. A disturbed soul could be one that has just developed a dented relationship with God through sin or an attack from the devil or an uncomfortable situation from another man or a mere negative circumstance (situation).
3. Anytime your soul is disturbed try and search for the cause by meditating on God's Word and believing Him to reveal it to you. Knowing the cause can help resolve it to a large extent.
4. Irrespective of how worried you are, constantly put your hope and trust in God.
5. Focus on (the goodness of) God rather than the situation. Perceive that God is well able to turn the situation around for your advantage.
6. Another strategy to handle a worried soul is by constantly praising God (inwardly and/or outwardly), for God inhabits the praises of His people.
7. When we praise God even during our disturbed situations, He manifests Himself in our troubles and gives us solutions.

Prayer: Dear God, when my soul is overwhelmed with troubles lead me to the Rock (Jesus) Who is higher than I (Psalm 61:2).

What action(s) will I take today to improve my life?

_____

_____

_____

_____

January 16

You are not Insignificant

Scripture reading: Exodus 3:1-12

Exodus 3:11-12
But Moses said to God, "Who am I that I should go to Pharaoh, and that I should bring the children of Israel out of Egypt?" So He said, "I will certainly be with you. And this shall be a sign to you that I have sent you: when you have brought the people out of Egypt, you shall serve God on this mountain."

1. God has bestowed on us (Christians) such great blessings that we should desist from belittling ourselves.
2. If you do not know how special and powerful God has made you, you tend to allow circumstances to negatively dictate to you and people to underestimate your potentials.
3. Belittling ourselves hurts God because we belittle Him as well (in the process).
4. When you know the Big God who resides in you, you will place great value on yourself and accomplish greater things to His glory; because you are His offspring.
5. Always remember God's promise: "I will never leave you nor forsake you". This will always give you the confidence to progress in life; because He's always with us if we constantly remain in Him.
6. You can know more about what God has deposited in you and what you are capable of by daily spending time with His Word (The Bible). The Bible will reveal the secrets to a successful good life.
7. When God gives you an assignment, ask Him for grace and the wisdom to accomplish it, instead of looking at your incapability.

Prayer: Heavenly Father, give me the foresight to understand how great You have made me. Let me never again underestimate Your power which lives in me. In Jesus' Name!

What action(s) will I take today to improve my life?

_____

_____

_____

_____

If a man does only what is required of him, he is a slave.
The moment he does more, he is a free man

Harry Lorayne (Secrets of Mind Power)

January 17

Be a Source of Encouragement to Others

Scripture reading: 1 John 1:1-4

1 John 1:4
And these things we write to you that your joy may be full.

1. Develop the culture of giving people hope via the Word of God by speaking, writing or living/demonstrating it.
2. Instead of making the lives of others miserable through your mannerisms, attitudes and actions, give them encouragement.
3. When you give people hope they become joyful and are to live successfully.
4. There are many people that due to unpleasant life experiences never felt loved. Aim to put a smile on the faces of people for you may not know those who need it.
5. Joy is the fuel for the soul, which resultantly affects the body as well. A joyful soul leads to a happy and healthy body.
6. God desires that our joy may be full. That is why He's forever attentive to our prayers and willing to answer them. That is why He wants us to always do His will (or please Him) so He can continue to bless us.
7. When your encouragement and giving of hope spur people unto better lives it gives you joy and fulfillment.

Prayer: Dear Jesus, let me be a source of encouragement to others so that through You I can give them hope for the future.

What action(s) will I take today to improve my life?

_____

_____

_____

_____

January 18

You are Seated with Christ in Heavenly Places

Scripture reading: Ephesians 2:1-10

Ephesians 2:6
And raised us up together, and made us sit together in the heavenly places in Christ Jesus.

1. When Christ died on the cross we died with Him; our sinful nature died with Him on the cross.
2. When Christ resurrected from the dead we resurrected with Him; our spirit was made whole again so we can have a relationship with God (and directly go to God at all times).
3. When God resurrected us with Christ He raised us up to be seated with Him (Christ) in the heavenly places.
4. If God has placed us in heavenly places, then we have the power to rule the first and second heavens; that is the atmosphere and the demonic or spiritual world.
5. The truth is that, if we are seated with Christ and the devil fears Him, then Satan fears us too. Satan scares us sometimes because we fail to know, understand and/or believe this truth. He therefore capitalizes on our ignorance and puts fear into us.
6. Because God has raised us with Christ to heavenly places we can do greater works as Christ promised in John 14:12.
7. We can fully express our authority over the heavenly places only if we continue to dwell in Christ Jesus and live according to The Word.

Prayer: Thank You LORD for letting me know that I am seated in heavenly places with Christ Jesus. By faith, I exercise the authority You have given me over every situation, whether physical or spiritual. In Jesus' mighty Name. Amen.

What action(s) will I take today to improve my life?

_____

_____

_____

_____

January 19

God's Worker on Earth

Scripture reading: Ephesians 2:10-22

Ephesians 2:10
For we are His workmanship, created in Christ Jesus for good works, which God prepared beforehand that we should walk in them.

1. We are the handiwork of God. Everything that God does is excellent; therefore He has made us excellent.
2. The excellent nature God has made us can be fully realized when we acknowledge it and work towards maintaining it.
3. We have also been made/created in Christ Jesus. We have the attitude and mind of Christ. We should never allow Satan to deceive or manipulate us. It also means we are protected in and by Christ.
4. Since Christ did good works, we should also act similarly because we live in Him.
5. Good works is demonstrating the commands/instructions in the Bible. It is listening to the Holy Spirit and obeying Him at all times. It is becoming a blessing to people.
6. God has given everyone some form of assignment to complete. It is your responsibility to identify, pursue and accomplish them. When you accomplish the works then you are living a well fulfilled life.
7. It is when we do these good works that we are expressing the nature of God or Christ that is in us.

Prayer: Dear God, please let me avail my life for you so You can use me for good works.

What action(s) will I take today to improve my life?

_____

_____

_____

_____

January 20

Restored Joy

Scripture reading: Psalm 51:1-13

Psalm 51:12
Restore to me the joy of Your salvation. And uphold me by Your generous Spirit.

1. One of the greatest gifts one can lack is the joy of God's salvation. Even the Christian can be in need of it if the individual does not know his/her position in Christ.
2. It is God's joy of salvation that gives us joy in Him. It means salvation in God through Christ is the foundation of joy.
3. The Christian may lack the joy typically when he is detached from God, particularly due to sin/disobedience or ignorance.
4. Never allow the joy of God to elude you. When you lose it as a result of committing even the worst of sins do not remain idle. Come back to God for forgiveness so that He can restore you.
5. Remember it is the joy of the LORD that gives us strength; without it we cannot progress in our Christian walk.
6. The joy of the LORD sustains and keeps us in our relationship with God. It fuels our faith and gives us the courage to stand against the wiles of the devil.
7. Satan will always deceive you that your sin is so great to warrant God's forgiveness. God is forever ready to forgive you if you humbly ask for it (1 John 1:9).

Prayer: Heavenly Father, no matter what I'm going through please restore to me the joy of Your salvation so I can have strength to carry on. In Jesus' Name. Amen.

What action(s) will I take today to improve my life?

_____

_____

_____

_____

January 21

Panaceas for Worry

Scripture reading: Matthew 6:25-34

Philippians 4:6
Be anxious for nothing, but in everything by prayer and supplication, with thanksgiving, let your requests be made known to God.

1. Worry or anxiety has no benefit. It only increases the adrenalin level, excess of which can cause long term undue stresses and cardiovascular problems.
2. Anxiety has never improved any situation; it rather prevents you from thinking productively for solutions. Both positive and negative thoughts cannot prevail in your mind at the same time. When anxious thoughts prevail productive ones cannot (and vice versa).
3. When you become anxious you give the devil the opportunity to put doubts and fear in your mind, which can cause more anxiety and disbelief in the promises of God concerning your life.
4. Invariably, not all anxious thoughts are real; some are only imaginative, but so powerful to harm a person.
5. Convert all your anxieties into prayer, worship, praises, thanksgiving to God; and also into productive thinking.
6. Prayer of worship, praises and thanksgiving wards off anxiety. It helps you to shift focus from the problem so you can concentrate in finding solutions rather than worrying. It also glorifies God so He moves in His power on your behalf.
7. Instead of worrying talk to God for solutions and He will speak back to you.

Prayer: Instead of focusing on the problems, may I always look up to You, Jesus, in my anxious moments.

What action(s) will I take today to improve my life?

_____
_____
_____
_____

January 22

The Foundation of Life

Scripture reading: Matthew 7:24-29

Matthew 7:24-25
"Therefore whoever hears these sayings of Mine, and does them, I will liken him to a wise man who built his house on the rock: and the rain descended, the floods came, and the winds blew and beat on that house; and it did not fall, for it was founded on the rock.

1. The benefits derived from the Word of God for prosperity can be obtained by anyone who hears His words and puts them into practice; whether Christian, Muslim, Hindu, pagan, atheist etc. The principles of life in the Bible works for everyone.
2. Without hearing you can never know and consequently have no avenue to put it into practice.
3. You must therefore develop the attitude of reading, studying, meditating and hearing the Word of God at all times. That is why you should always have your quiet time daily and also be in the assembly of believers; be in a Bible believing church.
4. Knowing the Word is one level, putting it into practice gives it value and expression. Deriving the benefits of the Word of God is a process of knowing and doing; knowledge in action.
5. The one who puts the Word into practice is the wise person, because he makes good use of the knowledge.
6. If the one who hears the Word and fails to apply them is a foolish person, how much more the one who does not hear it at all?
7. The Word of God is our foundation for life and prosperity. It gives us the backbone to face every challenge in life so we can become successful.
8. Always build up yourself with God's Word for you do not know when the difficult times will come. When those times come it is the level/measure of God's Word in you that will determine whether you will be able to stand.

Prayer: God, please help me to put Your Word into practice so I will be wiser. In Jesus' Name I pray. Amen.

What action(s) will I take today to improve my life?

_____

_____

_____

_____

January 23

Always Give Glory to God

Scripture reading: Judges 7:1-25

Judges 7:2
And the LORD said to Gideon, "The people who are with you are too many for Me to give the Midianites into their hands, lest Israel claim glory for itself against Me, saying, 'My own hand has saved me.'

1. The LORD is always speaking to us in one way or the other; we have to be constantly attentive and obedient.
2. God does not deal with the numbers/majority but the availability, preparedness and commitment of people.
3. Usually involving all and sundry in a pursuit can lead to failure due to the possibility of indifference and discouraging attitudes of the masses.
4. Usually God will cause all your hopes on people, money, strength, beauty etc. to be lost so that when He grants you victory you will have no cause to attribute it to anyone or anything but Him.
5. Never try to take God's glory. It can be very deadly. God does not share His glory with anyone. Give all praise and glory back to Him.
6. When you claim glory for yourself you are literally fighting God. It is tantamount to becoming God's enemy.
7. Even when it seems it was your own intensive preparation or great efforts that gave you success, remember God gave you life in order to use your efforts. Ultimately, every success is linked to God's free provision of life.

Prayer: My heavenly Father, please do not let me be puffed-up when praise is being given to me. Let me always give glory to you in all my endeavors.

What action(s) will I take today to improve my life?

_____

_____

_____

_____

A successful person is one who finds what God intend for him to do with his life, prepares himself to do it, and does it daily to the best of his ability

Jim Davidson (How to Plan Your Life)

January 24

Give God your Lifetime

Scripture reading: Psalm 31:1-18

Psalm 31:15
My times are in Your hand; deliver me from the hand of my enemies, and from those who persecute me.

1. When God created man He gave man his own will.
2. Adam (man) naturally knew what was good only until he disobeyed God and found out the option to do bad things as well. Man therefore obtained the ability to choose between good and evil.
3. God cannot force man to worship Him. It is in man's will to either choose or refuse to serve God.
4. Until man decides to give his will (i.e. both good and bad aspects of his life) back to God he cannot enjoy the fullness of God.
5. Time is life. It is God who has given us life and consequently time as well. Our time is therefore God's time and our life is also God's life.
6. Many Christians have given their life to Christ but have not given their time to Him. They seem so busy (even for the work of God) that they do not make time for God; they do not have a consistent personal relationship with Him.
7. Always ensure you give your time to God. When you give your time to God it implies you have given your ways to Him.
8. Give your lifetime to God and He will take care of you at all times.

Prayer: Thank you LORD for having me inscribed in the palms of Your hands. I thank You that my days are in Your hands.

What action(s) will I take today to improve my life?

_____
_____
_____
_____

January 25

Just Trust and Obey

Scripture reading: John 9:1-11

John 9:7
And He said to him, "Go, wash in the pool of Siloam" (which is translated, Sent). So he went and washed, and came back seeing.

1. God always speaks to us in many situations. It is up to us to be attentive, receptive and obedient.

2. Usually many of the instructions from God do not seem logical, but they pay off greatly if we heed to and act on them. For the things of the Spirit of God seem foolish to the natural person (mind) because man uses his mind instead of using his spiritual understanding (1 Corinthians 2:14).

3. When we go to God we should not allow our preconceived minds to be superior to the instructions/commands He gives us. Our expectations can deceive us and make us miss God's timing or instructions. The blind man I suppose expected Christ to touch his eyes for his healing. He may have been surprised and/or disappointed initially, however he obeyed Christ's instructions.

4. Go to the LORD with an opened mind, ready to take any of His instructions.

5. Sometimes the things we consider worthless, can be the source of our breakthrough.

6. God is not so concerned about our "extraordinary efforts" or our logical reasoning but our obedience. Obedience is indeed better than sacrifice.

7. We should always seek to obey God's instructions irrespective of how illogical it may be. This is what will give us great results.

8. Another way to say this is: Take the Word of the LORD just as it is.

9. The Word of the LORD gives us the opportunity to walk by faith.

Prayer: Oh LORD! Your Word is indeed the ultimate instruction for success. Please give me the heart to believe every Word of Yours so I can realize great results.

What action(s) will I take today to improve my life?

_____

_____

_____

_____

January 26

Act What You Say

Scripture reading: 1 John 3:13-24

1 John 3:18
Dear children, let us not love with words or speech but with actions and in truth.

1. God wants us to receive His Word as little children who are readily receptive to His teachings.
2. To love is a verb, an action/a doing phrase, not an abstract thing. It should therefore be demonstrated in deeds/works but not in words only.
3. As much as the express evidence of a verb is in its action, we must express love in action.
4. We should convert our good words into good deeds and be truthful in our speech.
5. It is only when we act on what we say that we become truthful to our words and earn the trust of others.
6. The person who is committed to his word usually starts or accomplishes a task before he begins to talk about it.
7. We should do more but talk less. Be a doer, not a talker.
8. The more you talk, the more you are bound to make unrealistic promises (which cannot be fulfilled), and people may see you as a liar.
9. The more we talk we become boastful; and God demotes the proud.

Prayer: Let me become a practical Christian; one who puts Your Word into action at all times. Please help me to demonstrate Your love towards others, to bring them to Your saving grace.

What action(s) will I take today to improve my life?

_____

_____

_____

_____

January 27

Open Up to God's Word

Scripture reading: Luke 3:1-9

Luke 3:2b
During the high-priesthood of Annas and Caiaphas, the word of God came to John son of Zechariah in the wilderness.

1. The Word of God is the source of life, peace and success on earth. It cannot be dealt away with.
2. The Word of God is Jesus Christ Himself (John 1:1-2, 14).
3. The Word of God is no respecter of persons. God can bypass the pastor and speak to a new convert in the church. You therefore do not need to be a priest to hear God's Word.
4. Always deem it important to receive God's Word at any time or in any situation; whether it's for edification, instruction, teaching, correction or rebuke.
5. Always create the atmosphere to receive God's Word because He always has something new/fresh for your day.
6. Be ready to receive God's Word in any form: audibly from Him, prophecy, reading, hearing from someone or electronically.
7. God is always speaking to us; however, much depends on our availability, sensitivity and receptiveness.
8. Sometimes you will hear God speak most of the time during your wilderness experience. Use your wilderness experience (i.e. the difficult times) to hear from Him instead of constantly complaining.

Prayer: Dear Father, I thank You that You are a speaking God. I bless You that You are always speaking. Please help me to exercise a sensitive and receptive spirit to receive Your Word. In Jesus' precious Name I pray. Amen.

What action(s) will I take today to improve my life?

_____

_____

_____

_____

January 28

Be a Channel of Comfort

Scripture reading: John 11:17-37

John 11:19
And many Jews had come to Martha and Mary to comfort them in the loss of their brother.

1. One of the tragic loss to man is the death of a loved one.
2. Everybody needs somebody at one point in life or the other because no one is an island.
3. You may not realize the importance of the people around you until you are in need or calamity befalls you.
4. There are some things that money cannot buy; one of them is the presence of genuine care and comfort from people.
5. If you want to be liked, be likeable. If you want to be loved, be loveable. Build healthy relationships at all times for you do not know when you will need people.
6. When you build good relationship and you lose a loved one you will most likely receive comfort from people.
7. Learn how to genuinely comfort people by empathizing with them; show care and concern as if you are in their situation.
8. When we give comfort to people we lighten their problems and give them strength to go through the difficulties.
9. Comfort from man is good but the greatest comfort can be received only from God, through the Holy Spirit. When all the "comforters" leave your house later in the day, you will be left alone; then the only One who can still be with you is the Holy Spirit. He is indeed our Comforter.

Prayer: Heavenly Father, please give me a heart of concern for others. Let me be a channel of comfort to the broken-hearted.

What action(s) will I take today to improve my life?

_____

_____

_____

_____

January 29

Declare the Glory of God

Scripture reading: Psalm 96:1-13

Psalm 96:3
Declare his glory among the nations, His marvelous deeds among all peoples.

1. It is the duty of the Christian to declare the glory of God to the world and to the people who are far and near.
2. The LORD has done so much for you that you shouldn't withhold the glory due Him.
3. The glory of the LORD is His goodness (marvelous deeds). Since God has been good to you (at least by giving you the gift of life) then you have cause to give him glory.
4. Declaring God's glory is praising/boasting about Him for the wonders He has done in your life.
5. God expects that we talk about His goodness to others so they believe in Him also and come to the saving knowledge of Jesus Christ.
6. These days it is even easier to declare God's glory through several platforms: social media (emails, Facebook, Twitter, WhatsApp etc.), text messages, church bulletins, posters etc.
7. When you declare God's glory you are literally telling Him you appreciate His goodness and you trust that He will do more.
8. Any time you refuse to declare God's glory you fail to appreciate His goodness. You limit open doors for your future.

Prayer: Cause me to love to praise you at all times, oh LORD. Anywhere I find myself, let me continue to declare Your glory. Amen.

What action(s) will I take today to improve my life?

_____

_____

_____

_____

January 30

Carry your Cross

Scripture reading: Luke 14:25-34

Luke 14:27
And whoever does not carry their cross and follow me cannot be my disciple.

1. Christianity is not bread and butter. Everyone has his/her own cross to carry.
2. Your "cross" could mean a challenge or difficulty or burden you may be going through.
   It could be your goal in life that you want to accomplish; which has become a burden on your heart.
3. It could also be something/someone dear to you (that you cherish so much) that could come between you and God (and mar the relationship).
4. To carry your cross simply means, to die to self (and self-ambition) and live for Christ- to sacrifice.
5. You must always put God first in order to carry your cross; otherwise you do not qualify to be His disciple.
6. Remember your cross is part of the Christian race. If you put God first He will help you to deal with it.
7. To carry your cross, therefore, also means putting God first in all you do and fully obeying His Law/Word despite your situation, hardship or aspirations.
8. We have to follow Christ at all times and in all situations.

Prayer: I have no power of my own. Give me grace LORD to carry my cross so I can be Your disciple. Amen.

What action(s) will I take today to improve my life?

_____

_____

_____

_____

To look is one thing
To see what you look at is another
To understand what you see is a third
To learn from what you understand is still something else
But to act on what you learn is all that really matters

Harry Lorayne (Secrets of Mind Power)

January 31

Pride yourself in the Cross

Scripture reading: Galatians 6:12-16

Galatians 6:14
May I never boast except in the cross of our Lord Jesus Christ, through which the world has been crucified to me, and I to the world.

1. Some Christians boast in themselves concerning the works God has wrought in their lives instead of praising/boasting in God.
2. The person who boasts about him/herself is gradually digging his/her own pit. For God resists and demotes the proud.
3. Anytime you pride in yourself you indirectly tell God that you are self-sufficient and do not acknowledge His presence in your life.
4. Christians should rather boast in God by praising Him. We should brag about the marvelous things God has done in our lives. In so doing, we make Christ known to the world so it may accept His salvation.
5. The cross is the only basis for our Christianity and it's the most important foundation. The products of the cross are the victorious life the Christian leads. Therefore he can boast about the products of the cross.
6. The products of the cross include freedom from Satan's control/influence, deliverance from generational curses, joy, peace and sense of purpose in life.
7. Paul was describing being part of the crucifixion; crucified with Christ through the tribulations he went through.
8. "The world should be crucified to you"– the characteristics of the world must be dead in you; i.e. nothing of the world should be found in you.
9. "You must be crucified to the world"– you should be dead to the things of the world such that you should not respond to its desires when given to you even on a golden platter.

10. You can say the above confidently after you have gone through the wilderness experience.

Prayer: Dear Jesus, let me always remember the cross as the foundation of my new life. Give me the grace to boast in You rather than in myself. Thank You LORD for this grace. Amen.

What action(s) will I take today to improve my life?

_____
_____
_____
_____

February 1

God's Forgiving Power

Scripture reading: 1 John 1:3-10

1 John 1:9
If we confess our sins, He is faithful and just to forgive us our sins and to cleanse us from all unrighteousness.

1. If we ask for God's forgiveness, He will definitely forgive us. When God forgives us He does not remember it anymore. It is as though we never sinned.
2. However, do not make it a habit to continue to live in sin; considering that you do not know when you may not have another chance to confess because death comes without a warning. Also, you do not know when the devil may eventually grip you such that you may not have the conviction or opportunity to confess; i.e. when you reach a state of apostasy.
3. Do not allow the devil to make you feel worthless because of your past sins or mistakes.
4. When you know God's forgiving power the devil cannot use your past against you.
5. The God of forgiveness is the same God of judgment. Remember that the same God who can forgive you can also punish you when the time is due.
6. It is the shedding of the blood of Jesus that purifies us from all sins.
7. When God forgives you He can also give you the power to overcome the sin. Therefore, when you ask for forgiveness also ask Him to deliver you from that power of sin.

Prayer: Heavenly Father, I thank You for the power of Your forgiveness. Please give me the strength to overcome every influence of sin. In Jesus' mighty Name. Amen.

What action(s) will I take today to improve my life?

_____
_____
_____
_____

February 2

The Power of the Resurrection

Scripture reading: Romans 6:1-14

Romans 6:8-9
Now if we died with Christ, we believe that we shall also live with Him, knowing that Christ, having been raised from the dead, dies no more. Death no longer has dominion over Him.

1. The mystery of the cross is that when Christ died we (Christians) died with him. When He resurrected we resurrected with Him as well.
2. When we died with Christ, our sins were buried with Him. Therefore, if we are still sinning we must check our hearts whether we have truly given our entire life to Him. We must make sure we have allowed Him to deal with every power of sin that resides in us.
3. As a Christian you are now living with and for Christ and dead to sin.
4. If we are living with Christ then we have to do His work and live His kind of life.
5. If we are living with Christ then we should be in tune (or right standing) with Him. Then Satan will fear us as he fears Him.
6. If we are living with Christ then we should live a victorious life.
7. If death and Satan has no mastery over Christ then we should not allow him to have mastery over us.

Prayer: Always take me back to the cross, dear LORD, where You delivered me from the power of sin, so I can continually live for You.

What action(s) will I take today to improve my life?

_____
_____
_____
_____

February 3

Obedience for Success

Scripture reading: Exodus 15:22-27

Exodus 15:25a
So he cried out to the Lord, and the Lord showed him a tree. When he cast it into the waters, the waters were made sweet.

1. God is always speaking. You can perceive His voice particularly when you acknowledge His presence in your ways.
2. Many of God's blessings are conditional and they are hinged on our obedience to His commands (Word).
3. God commands that we listen to Him at all times.
4. We should not just hear God speak, but we should carefully listen to Him. Hearing and listening are totally different.
5. When we listen to God (or His Word) it is not enough. We must also do what He says. We keep His statutes by doing His will.
6. One constant way we can listen to God is to continually read His Word- The Bible.
7. We must always do what is right in the sight of God, not in our sight.
8. Some things may be right in our own eyes but wrong in God's sight. Other things may seem right in accordance to the Bible but if done at a wrong time, the action and motive becomes wrong as well.
9. If it is not right in God's sight then it is not worth doing. When it is right in God's sight, it does not matter what the world says.
10. When we do God's will He protects us from all diseases. Mind you, living healthily is also part of keeping God's will, "Your body is the temple of the LORD"

Prayer: Heavenly Father, help me to be sensitive to Your voice. Please give me a heart of obedience in order to do Your will.

What action(s) will I take today to improve my life?

_____

_____

_____

_____

February 4

True Love

Scripture reading: 1 Corinthians 13:1-13

1 Corinthians 13:7-8a
Love bears all things, believes all things, hopes all things, endures all things. Love never fails.

1. Love is a humungous topic because it is a major foundation of our lives. It can never be exhausted; no man can wholly define it. This is also because the source of true love is God.
2. "Love bears all things" – Love is resilient; tough; can resist all pressure; cannot break. Love never gives up.
3. "Love believes all things" – Love has a strong faith or a strong level of trust in worthy things. It has strong belief system, particularly in God and the things of God.
4. "Love hopes all things" – Love has the strong hope that God will turn things right at the right time.
5. "Love endures all things" – This is related to "Love bears all things".
6. "Love never fails" – Love does not disappoint. Love is always trustworthy.
7. As people of God we should spur on to emulate and demonstrate these qualities of love in our daily lives.
8. If you lack any of these love qualities ask God to endue you with it.

Prayer: Your love is everlasting and always reliable. It supersedes every other love. LORD please create in me a heart of true love.

What action(s) will I take today to improve my life?

_____

_____

_____

_____

February 5

Be Aggressive to Overcome the Devil

Scripture reading: Matthew 11:2-15

Matthew 11:12
And from the days of John the Baptist until now the kingdom of heaven suffers violence, and the violent take it by force.

1. The kingdom of God is not bread and butter. It is a battle. Having this awareness will enable you avoid potential failures in life.
2. The devil is constantly wrestling against the plans of God for your life. He is constantly and violently fighting against Christians so that God's plans could be curtailed.
3. John the Baptist is a representation of the demonstration of fierceness in the kingdom of God and the passion for expansion of God's kingdom right here on earth.
4. Many are the implicit and explicit promises of God concerning your life but you can access them by force with determination through consistent prayer and right application of God's Word.
5. You have to aggressively take up your blessings in God before you can experience it because on the other side of the coin is Satan fighting against you.
6. Every Christian has his/her own battle at one point or the other. You should recognize these specific battles and wage spiritual war against them. Take action of your battles.
7. God is always waiting for you to wrestle the spiritual wars so He can grant you victory.
8. Key action words: Violent, fierce, passionate, zeal, aggressive, determine and bold. You need these to keep Satan where he belongs.

Prayer: I command every satanic activity to be destroyed from my life. I possess everything God has promised me right now in Jesus' Mighty Name. Amen.

What action(s) will I take today to improve my life?

_____

_____

_____

_____

February 6

Seek God Everywhere

Scripture reading: Psalm 61:1-8

Psalm 61:2
From the end of the earth I will cry to You. When my heart is overwhelmed; lead me to the rock that is higher than I.

1. God is Omnipresent. Do not wait to get to church before trying to reach out to God. Wherever you find yourself you can seek Him.
2. Even when you find yourself in an ungodly place, come to this realization that you can seek God to take you out of that ungodly situation.
3. God is ever ready waiting for you to call upon Him.
4. When things are so hard and gloomy and your heart is overwhelmed such that there is no way you can handle it, take it to the LORD in prayer.
5. When the enemy encompasses you to bring you shame and destruction cry out to God in prayer and trust Him to deliver you.
6. One way troubles make your heart faint is when Satan makes you feel that God cannot help you this time. He puts doubts into your mind and if your heart accepts it then your faith is weakened. Therefore, when you feel overwhelmed by troubles meditate on God's Word to build up your faith so you can go through the situation victoriously.
7. The Rock— Christ Jesus is the Solid Rock. He is the incomparable high power. A power higher than you and higher/bigger than all your challenges.

Prayer: You are My Rock; my fortress and hiding place. In my distressful moments I run to You for refuge. Thank You Jesus for always being there for me.

What action(s) will I take today to improve my life?

_____

_____

_____

_____

Logic produces sequence and order, but your faith produces miracles

Mike Murdock (Seeds of Wisdom)

February 7

Build Up Your Faith

Scripture reading: Mark 5:21-34

Mark 5:27-28
When she heard about Jesus, she came behind Him in the crowd and touched His garment. For she said, "If only I may touch His clothes, I shall be made well."

1. After seeking all possible solutions this woman still decided to seek Jesus.
2. She never allowed her past (disappointments, discouragements, delays and shame) to prevent her from receiving her miracle.
3. Touching the garment of Jesus was a strong level of faith.
4. She already had the faith before she went to Jesus; because she had already heard about Him. The sharing of your miracle will build the faith of another person.
5. She had to make her way through the crowd, through the challenges, before getting to her breakthrough. She actually broke through her challenges.
6. Believe strongly in God that He is able to do all things.
7. Do not wait for your pastor to lay hands on you before you can receive your miracle. You can initiate your own miracle.
8. How can people hear about Jesus in order to seek Him? We must talk about Jesus to the people of the world.

Prayer: In the Name of Jesus I receive the grace to increase the level of my faith. From hence forth, no matter my challenges I will constantly depend on God.

What action(s) will I take today to improve my life?

_____
_____
_____
_____

February 8

Pursue Great Virtues

Scripture reading: 2 Timothy 2:20-26

2 Timothy 2:22
Flee also youthful lusts; but pursue righteousness, faith, love, peace with those who call on the Lord out of a pure heart.

1. Sin must not be entertained at all. Immediately you perceive its presence just flee from it or avoid it.
2. The youth is more prone to evil desires because they are more adventurous and have a lot of exuberance.
3. One easy way to be attracted to evil desires is being idle or doing something unproductive or unconnected to your purpose. Have you realized that anytime you go online without a definite purpose, you browse unnecessarily and go to unproductive sites which can cause you to indulge in sinful and unhealthy habits?
4. Another way to be attracted to evil desires is irresponsibility and lack of self-control. You must take charge of your life to decide what you want to influence you.
5. When you constantly pursue righteousness, evil thoughts and desires will be distant from you. It is about having and pursuing a definite purpose that glorifies God.
6. Pursue good virtues such as righteousness, faith, love and peace.
7. A healthy environment to cultivate these virtues is the church and among Christians. However, you usually exhibit these virtues in the outside world. It is the world that tests the strength of your virtues.
8. Above all, always strive to have a pure heart. Anytime you realize your heart is impure check your environment and the things you feed your eyes and mind with.
9. The perfect method to keep a pure heart is through the Word of God and prayer. It is knowing and doing what the Word says.

Prayer: Dear LORD. Help me to overcome all (enticing) sin but to pursue all acts of godliness. Amen.

What action(s) will I take today to improve my life?

_____

_____

_____

_____

February 9

Spiritual Exchange by Faith

Scripture reading: Galatians 3:1-14

Galatians 3:13
Christ has redeemed us from the curse of the law, having become a curse for us (for it is written, "Cursed is everyone who hangs on a tree").

1. Just as Haman wanted to hang Mordecai on the pole because he wanted to disgrace Mordecai and the Israelites (through the curse of hanging on the tree), so also Christ became a curse for us by allowing Himself to be hung on a tree (i.e. the cross).
2. When we accepted Christ the curse of sin was taken away from us (because He bore our sin).
3. To redeem is to deliver one from a negative situation to a positive one; death to life, poverty to riches, sickness to health, and disappointment to favor. It comes with a price. Christ bought us with the highest price– His precious blood.
4. Jesus became every negative pattern that you experience in your life on the cross so that you may experience joy and peace. This is the spiritual beneficial exchange Christ gave us. It is one thing to know this; it is another to appropriate it in your life.
5. You can appropriate and experience this spiritual exchange by believing that Christ took away all your troubles and by also speaking (prayers and confessions) to that trouble and commanding it (by the Word of the LORD) out of your life.
6. You should value the price at which you have been bought. Do not take it for granted. Do not continue to sin because grace abound.
7. The curse of the law: Those who perceive that their redemption or salvation is based on the law. The law requires that you save yourself by good works (which is impossible), faith in Christ requires that you are saved through grace.

Prayer: Thank You Jesus for taking away the curse and replacing it with abundant blessings.

What action(s) will I take today to improve my life?

_____

_____

_____

_____

February 10

Make Prayer a Lifestyle

Scripture reading: Luke 18:1-8

Luke 18:1
Then He spoke a parable to them, that men always ought to pray and not lose heart.

1. Prayer should not be made seasonally. It should be continuous. It should be a lifestyle.
2. If you recognize that prayer is communication to and from God, you will always pray. This is because you should always be talking to/with God. That is why your quiet time is very important. You should daily observe it.
3. The reason prayer is seasonal for many is that we tend to pray only when we are in trouble or in need. It is as though we have made God a spare tire; we only need Him when we get a flat tire.
4. When prayer becomes a lifestyle you need not do any extraordinary/special prayer in times of trouble. The Holy Spirit will lead you to pray over a particular matter even before it happens.
5. When prayer becomes a lifestyle God even perceives your conversations, declarations or sometimes your thoughts (in your heart) as prayer and honors them.
6. If you have been praying about a particular matter and it is still pending, do not lose heart. Continue to pray.
7. When prayer becomes a lifestyle, praying over a particular matter over and over again does not become a burden; so you do not give up. Because you know one day it will surely come to pass.

Prayer: Dear Father, please cause me to develop a constant prayer relationship with You. No matter the toughness of a situation teach me to persist in my supplications.

What action(s) will I take today to improve my life?

_____

_____

_____

_____

February 11

God's Word for Your Life is Sure

Scripture reading: Luke 1:26-38

Luke 1:37
For with God nothing will be impossible.

1. God's Word is supreme. It supersedes every law or decree.
2. God has the power to fulfill His Word regardless of every difficulty.
3. Let this scripture speak to your spirit (heart) and mind that: "whatever God has spoken concerning your life will surely come to pass".
4. When you receive God's Word accept and believe it like a little child.
5. When God's Word comes to you do not look at your circumstances or limitations. Accept the Word and believe that it will surely come to pass. Commit yourself to it to see it manifest. That is, do what He has asked you in order to see it come through.
6. Invariably, the Word of God comes with some commandments you need to obey. If you do your part it will come to pass.
7. It is in only very few cases that you only have to believe and do nothing else. Even in such cases of belief you have to work it out in your spirit through consistent prayer and meditation. So we are always in partnership with God. God gives the Word, we commit ourselves to it by doing our part, and then He fulfills it.
8. If you always believe that God's Word will surely come to pass, you shall lack nothing.

Prayer: Increase my faith LORD in every situation so I can trust Your Word just as it is.

What action(s) will I take today to improve my life?

_____
_____
_____
_____

February 12

Learn to Live at Peace with People

Scripture reading: Matthew 5:21-26

Matthew 5:23-24
Therefore if you bring your gift to the altar, and there remember that your brother has something against you, leave your gift there before the altar, and go your way. First be reconciled to your brother, and then come and offer your gift.

1. As much as God first showed us how to love by loving us, He wants us to maintain a good relationship with people.
2. If we cannot love the people around us who we see, how can we love God Who we cannot physically see?
3. Obedience is better than sacrifice. Obedience is a gateway for us to offer sacrifices. Else, the sacrifices have no value. Obedience is the foundation on which sacrifices are made.
4. If we are not obedient to God then He does not need our sacrifice. If we cannot love those around us God is unhappy with us.
5. God values your relationship with people more than your gift to Him.
6. It is not a matter of you having a problem with the person but vice versa. It is your duty to reconcile even if you are not at fault.
7. The main point is that if you do not forgive your neighbor God cannot forgive you and answer your prayers.
8. Unforgiveness can really be a hindrance to your prayer.

Prayer: If I have harbored unforgiveness within me, Father help me to forgive. Amen.

What action(s) will I take today to improve my life?

_____
_____
_____
_____

February 13

Christ is the Power Who works through You

Scripture reading: Philippians 4:10-20

Philippians 4:13
I can do all things through Christ who strengthens me.

1. Paul is attributing all his achievements to Christ because He is his source of life.
2. God can help us do all things through Christ Jesus. He has given us divine ability to cause things to happen.
3. There is nothing that we cannot do when God is with us.
4. You can experience the power of Christ working within you by first of all accepting Him as your LORD.
5. Christ gives us strong faith and confidence if we totally depend on Him.
6. God has given us the ability to do anything that brings glory to His Name (John 14:12).
7. Even when you go through difficult times it is the power of God within you that will give you strength to overcome.
8. Although the power of God resides in you, until you acknowledge it you will not experience His strength.

Prayer: Praise be to You Jesus for giving me the divine ability to do things beyond my abilities. I am so blessed because You give me strength to carry on.

What action(s) will I take today to improve my life?

_____

_____

_____

_____

Always say less than necessary. Once the words are out, you cannot take them back. Keep them under control.

Robert Greene (48 Laws of Power)

February 14

Be Honest with Yourself

Scripture reading: Psalm 139:1-24

Psalm 139:23-24
Search me, O God, and know my heart. Try me, and know my anxieties. And see if there is any wicked way in me. And lead me in the way everlasting.

1. God knows us more than we know ourselves or anyone does.
2. God is the best Person who can correctly search our hearts. It is only Him who knows our hearts and thoughts.
3. As humans since we are bound to err we have to continually allow God to search through us so we can always be in His will.
4. To search one's heart is to be honest with one self. To be transparent and willing for every wrong intention to be exposed and to be willing to be corrected.
5. When God searches our hearts He is able to reveal every thought/intend which is ungodly.
6. It takes humility to allow one's self to be searched.
7. One human way of allowing one's self to be searched is being open to criticisms and corrections.
8. Pride, self-righteousness and self-deception are enemies that prevent you from allowing God to search your heart and thoughts.
9. A simple way to continually allow God to search you is through your daily quiet time (e.g. morning Bible devotion). It is during this moment that God exposes a wrong you committed the previous time so you may correct your ways.
10. The Word of God is the greatest means to search one's self.

Prayer: Search my innermost being Oh LORD and blot out any attitude that does not bring glory to you. Amen.

What action(s) will I take today to improve my life?

_____

_____

_____

_____

February 15

The Power of Words

Scripture reading: Numbers 14:26-38

Numbers 14:28
Say to them, 'As I live,' says the Lord, 'just as you have spoken in My hearing, so I will do to you.

1. Do not be on good terms with God only during good times. He is pleased when we still love and trust Him during hard times and He performs greater works in our lives.
2. Do not grumble or whine against the LORD when your request seems to be delaying. He is omniscient and will bring heart desire to pass in due course.
3. People hardly say "Thank you God" for each morning but nag almost all the time.
4. Instead of nagging you should rather praise God in all situations.
5. Never do anything that will incur the wrath of God, for no one can bare His wrath.
6. Be mindful of what you say. If you speak good things, God and His Angles take them and work it for your good. If you speak bad/evil things, Satan and his cohort (demons) take them and work it against you.
7. Respect the power of positive confession. The contrary is also true.

Prayer: LORD, train my tongue to speak words of hope and life. In my angry moments teach me to be calm so I do not speak any regrettable words.

What action(s) will I take today to improve my life?

_____

_____

_____

_____

February 16

Obedience to God Releases Blessing

Scripture reading: Luke 11:14-28

Luke 11:28
But He said, "More than that, blessed are those who hear the word of God and keep it!"

1. Blessings come from God and it comes through constant obedience to His Word.
2. Since the Word of God gives wisdom it is the foundation of blessing. Wisdom is the principal thing (Proverbs 4:7).
3. It is not enough to hear/listen to God's Word. It is more important to put it into practice (Philippians 4:9).
4. Being a Christian or having accepted Christ as LORD and Savior alone is not enough. You must obey or do His will to experience His blessings.
5. Many Christians hide behind being associated with a great man of God or a great church; however, they fail to follow the Word of God. Blessing is a mirage for such ones.
6. For you to enjoy life (and be happy) through the blessing of God you must fully obey His Word. Remember, it is the blessing of the LORD that makes you rich (Proverbs 10:22).
7. Repetition is the mother of practice, experience and perfection. What you listen to most often influences your life. Therefore when you constantly read and meditate on God's Word you have a greater tendency of putting it into practice.

Prayer: Thank You LORD that Your Word is the source of blessings. Help me to constantly put it into practice. In Jesus' Name. Amen.

What action(s) will I take today to improve my life?

_____

_____

_____

_____

February 17

The Word of God is Light

Scripture reading: Psalm 119:79-112

Psalm 119:105
Your word is a lamp to my feet and a light to my path.

1. The Word of God is the commandment, law and precepts God has given to man in order for us to walk in His will.
2. God's Word can also come directly to us through prophecy, dreams and trances. Sometimes, God's Word comes to us even through life experiences.
3. The Word of God is ultimately Jesus Christ Himself (John 1:1-2, 14-15).
4. God's Word is the ultimate guide for life; the manual for effective living.
5. God's Word gives us illumination. It opens our understanding to live effectively for God.
6. When we apply God's Word to our lives it lights our path. It shows us the right way to go and the right things to do.
7. It is only when we apply the Word to our lives that we activate its full benefit.

Prayer: I will always rely on Your Word for life's direction; for it is trustworthy.

What action(s) will I take today to improve my life?

_____
_____
_____
_____

February 18

The Power of Confessions

Scripture reading: 2 Corinthians 4:7-15

2 Corinthians 4:13
And since we have the same spirit of faith, according to what is written, "I believed and therefore I spoke," we also believe and therefore speak.

1. Do not get tired of quoting God's Word during situations. When you quote the Word to any situation or to the devil they obey. This means you constantly have to saturate your mind and spirit with God's Word.
2. We believe in our hearts and confess with our mouths.
3. When you believe the Word of God so much that it is imprinted/inscribed in your heart/spirit it gets to a stage where you cannot help it but to declare the Word.
4. The moment you believe a Word from God, begin to confess it. As you do so, it increases your faith more and more which in turns intensifies your confession.
5. Believing and confessing are cyclical. The more you demonstrate them they turn to increase. That is, confession feeds your faith and believing gives your confession clarity and alacrity.
6. Make confession another important value of your Christian life because Christianity is also about confessing/declaring/professing God's Word to situations.
7. Since we have the same Spirit we can make powerful, productive confessions/declarations like Isaiah, Elijah, Paul or even Jesus Himself; because He said greater works we will do if we believe Him (John 14:12).

Prayer: Increase my faith LORD anytime I encounter Your Word. Give me the boldness to declare Your Word at all times.

What action(s) will I take today to improve my life?

_____

_____

_____

_____

February 19

Be a Doer of the Word

Scripture reading: James 1:19-27

James 1:22
But be doers of the word, and not hearers only, deceiving yourselves.

1. It is good to listen to or read God's Word. However, if you do not apply it (i.e. do what it says) it becomes inefficient and you deceive yourself.
2. "Deceiving yourself" in this context means you are listening to the Word with no effort to apply it; you are making a public show of listening to the Word with no evidence of its impact.
3. Many Christians fail to apply God's Word because they do not take the pains to go through what it takes to have the Word imprinted in their hearts; they do not take time to study it. Some even read the Bible like a newspaper or novel.
4. For those who already know the Word but do not care to apply it, it is a great deception to them.
5. When you hear or read God's Word repeatedly and by constant meditation it is stored in your memory. When it fills your mind and you understand it, you begin to trust it; then your heart accepts and believes it. All these processes are possible by allowing the Holy Spirit who imprints it on your heart. When your heart accepts it and it overflows, with determination and purposefulness you start applying it to your life.
6. This is why it is important to have records of God's Word–preaching tapes, preaching notes, authored books etc.
7. The secret of a successful Christian is always doing what God's Word says.

Prayer: Dear Father, please give me a heart that yearns to listen to Your Word and the grace to apply it to my life.

What action(s) will I take today to improve my life?

_____

_____

_____

_____

February 20

Diversities Brings Uniqueness

Scripture reading: 1 Corinthians 12:12-26

1 Corinthians 12:12
For as the body is one and has many members, but all the members of that one body, being many, are one body, so also is Christ.

1. The Church, which is the body of Christ, has many segments (parts).
2. The segments may be with regards to differences in ideology or specific area of calling. This determines the primary focus of each denomination.
3. God allowed these diversities to make each one unique and so to meet the various needs of people.
4. The many segments is not a premise for arguments, divisions and disunity. So far as their foundation is Christ every church should be united for the common propagation of the gospel.
5. Even within a particular church there are groups and ministries because God has equipped everyone with a particular gift and at specific levels.
6. One gift is not superior over the other, no matter how charismatic it may be. We should therefore not disregard other's gift.
7. Every gift is needed for the growth of the church. When one gift which is perceived unimportant ceases to function it affects others, including the ones which seemed to be given much attention.

Prayer: Dear LORD, let us learn that our differences are present to complement each other. Help us to respect our diversities for out of which do we obtain strength.

What action(s) will I take today to improve my life?

_____
_____
_____
_____

The principle of affirmation says that, strong affirmative statements repeated continually in your conscious mind will inevitably be accepted as commands by your subconscious mind

Brian Tracy (Create Your Own Future)

February 21

The Word of God is Perfect

Scripture reading: Psalm 19:7-14

Psalm 19:7-8
The law of the Lord is perfect, converting the soul. The testimony of the Lord is sure, making wise the simple. The statutes of the Lord are right, rejoicing the heart. The commandment of the Lord is pure, enlightening the eyes.

1. The Law of the LORD is Jesus Christ. This means Jesus is perfect.
2. The Law is perfect when applied in the context of our personal relationship with Christ.
3. The Law does not work for those who live by it (with their own effort) in a religious way.
4. When you correctly apply the Law of the LORD it refreshes your soul by uplifting and revitalizing/energizing you to live victoriously for God.
5. The Law which is the Word of God is able to convert man (from his wicked ways) and guarantee him eternal life in heaven and a fulfilling life on earth.
6. Because the Word of God is perfect, it is trustworthy and never loses its relevance. You can trust it in every matter at any time.
7. The Word of God makes the one who lacks wisdom wise; and the one who yearns for more wisdom, wiser.
8. God's Word gives understanding to the simple. The simple is one who is not wise.
9. God's Word gives joy to the sad heart. The more you meditate on and trust in the Word, it gives you hope and gladdens your heart.

Prayer: Praise be to You LORD for Your perfect Word. In Your Word I am refreshed, enlightened and directed.

What action(s) will I take today to improve my life?

_____

_____

_____

_____

February 22

Continuous Joy

Scripture reading: Psalm 66:1-7

Philippians 4:4
Rejoice in the Lord always. Again I will say, rejoice!

1. To rejoice means to be joyful again and again. It means to make joy a continuous attitude which influences those who come around you.
2. Some people, including Christians, rejoice in the world, instead of in the LORD. They think gratifying fleshly desires is a way to make the soul happy. However, right after the "happy events" they recoil into their sorrowful, depressive life.
3. It is only when we rejoice in Christ that the vacuum in our soul can be filled.
4. You need to cultivate the attitude of being joyful because the joy of the LORD is your strength.
5. Be joyful at all times; both good times and bad times.
6. Jesus is our Prince of peace. He is our source of joy. When you have joy you are living the peace Christ has given. He gives us everlasting joy.
7. Ultimately, you can rejoice in the LORD only after you have made Jesus Christ the LORD of your life.

Prayer: During my difficult situations teach me to rejoice in You LORD. Cause my heart to overflow with Your joy so others will be blessed.

What action(s) will I take today to improve my life?

_____

_____

_____

_____

February 23

Rescue the Captives

Scripture reading: 2 Timothy 2:20-26

2 Timothy 2:26
And that they may come to their senses and escape the snare of the devil, having been taken captive by him to do his will.

1. It is our duty to preach the gospel to perishing souls; it is in God's power to bring them to repentance. However, until we preach to them God will not save them.
2. The devil uses "modern lifestyle" to take the youth as captives to do his will. This is because the youth are so adventurous but easily influenced.
3. Satan is capable of blindfolding people away from the Word of God, which is the Truth. When he blindfolds people Satan traps them by captivating their soul (i.e. mind, emotions and will). Until the light of God is shone on such ones, they will continue to do Satan's will.
4. Those who are going astray can come to their senses only when the Word of God is reiterated to them.
5. Due to Satan's blindfolding technique people do not realize they are on the path that leads to death. It is when we tell them about the Word of God that they can come to their senses to consider to live God's kind of life.
6. People do not realize they are on the path to destruction because the devil deceives them with the glamour of this world. That is why they need the light to expose the deceptions of Satan.
7. Usually, our lifestyle speaks volumes to unbelievers. We must live the Christ-like life so that others can watch us and desire to live God's kind of life by accepting Jesus Christ.

Prayer: Heavenly Father, I pray for the lives of those who are perishing. May Your Word reach them wherever they are to take off the deceptions of Satan from their eyes. In Jesus' Mighty Name. Amen.

What action(s) will I take today to improve my life?

_____

_____

_____

_____

February 24

Possess your Possessions

Scripture reading: Joshua 6-15

Joshua 14:12
Now therefore, give me this mountain of which the Lord spoke in that day; for you heard in that day how the Anakim were there, and that the cities were great and fortified. It may be that the Lord will be with me, and I shall be able to drive them out as the Lord said."

1. The promises of God are certainly for us to claim. If you do not claim them you cannot have them. And you should claim them NOW. That is faith.

2. We always have our part to play in claiming the promises of God. When we receive the promise we must fully believe it and carefully observe/obey the instructions that come with it.

3. No promise of God is on a silver platter. You must play your part by praying and calling it into being (i.e. the power of positive confession); and then taking every godly action associated with it.

4. Although Caleb was given the land (by Moses' declaration), he still had to fight the Anakites to possess it. We must 'fight' by God's power (faith) through prayer and commitment to possess our promises.

5. The factors (both physical and spiritual) that fight against our promises are numerous. Just as the land of the Anakites were fortified, until we fight we can never receive the manifestation of our promises.

6. Always write down God's promises concerning your life so you can remember and make reference to claim/demand it. If you do not write it down the tendency to forget is high. If you forget, then obviously you cannot claim it.

7. When you write or note down the promises of God you are committed to work towards bringing it to pass.

8. Any promise that does not manifest in your life is your fault because God is always faithful and committed to His promises.

Prayer: By faith I speak into every promise God has for my life, and I called them into being, right now. In Jesus' Name. Amen.

What action(s) will I take today to improve my life?

_____

_____

_____

_____

February 25

Always Live to Please Your LORD

Scripture reading: Colossians 2:6-15

Colossians 2:6-7
As you therefore have received Christ Jesus the Lord, so walk in Him, rooted and built up in Him and established in the faith, as you have been taught, abounding in it with thanksgiving.

1. The moment you receive Christ He becomes your LORD; so accord Him that recognition. For Christ to be your LORD, it means He is the owner of your life. You live for Him and not for yourself or someone else.
2. Some people receive Christ for Him to give them a good life, but not to be their LORD. They do not want to obey Him nor do His will. It cannot work out that way. When you come to Jesus He sets the rules not you.
3. In the same way, as you have received Christ as LORD allow Him to rule over your life according to His Word. The Christian life is not an erratic one; based on emotions and options. It is continually living for Christ Jesus.
4. A clear evidence of you as a Christian is living the Christ kind of life. You always seek to put aside your will and please Him only.
5. Living your life in Christ is not an event; it is a continuous, life-long practice.
6. The more you study and hear God's Word it establishes you in Him, builds you up and strengthens your faith.
7. When you are overflowed with God's Word daily you are always thankful in every situation.

Prayer: Thank You LORD that Your Word is the foundation of life. Give me the grace to live by it so I can fulfill Your purpose for my life.

What action(s) will I take today to improve my life?

_____

_____

_____

_____

February 26

God's Promises and its Manifestation

Scripture reading: 2 Corinthians 1:12-24

2 Corinthians 1:20
For all the promises of God in Him are Yes, and in Him Amen, to the glory of God through us.

1. The promises of God are the words that God has said concerning mankind. It can also be His words to mankind in general and to the church in particular. Others are still specific to individual Christians or group of Christians.
2. God may have given you many promises which seems overwhelming and inconsistent with your present situation. Irrespective of how many they are, your duty is to believe them and play your part of obedience to see them come to pass.
3. Man can promise and fail but God's promise is certain and sure.
4. "Yes" - God's promises and His response is one; they go together and are inseparable. When He gives His promise it is as though He's fulfilled it at that particular (immediate) moment. Sadly, what our eyes perceive is a time lag between the promise and its fulfilment (which is not in God's dictionary). Have the eyes of faith NOW!
5. "Through Him, the Amen…"- that's through Christ we declare faith. Therefore, you ask for the promises in God through Christ. You should also be in Christ in order to appropriate the promises which is evident in His blessings.
6. "Amen"- you must believe in God through faith that His Word will surely come true.
7. Eventually when the promise is fulfilled it brings glory to God. Always remember to give Him the glory.

Prayer: I believe in Your Word. I trust and depend on it. I declare that every promise of God concerning my life should come to pass in due season. Amen.

What action(s) will I take today to improve my life?

_____

_____

_____

_____

February 27

Possess Your Blessings by Faith

Scripture reading: Numbers 33:50-56

Numbers 33:53
You shall dispossess the inhabitants of the land and dwell in it, for I have given you the land to possess.

1. We live in an unfair world; a world full of enemies. If we do not always engage in battle the enemy will take us for a ride and we will not enjoy God's blessings.
2. God has given us the command to take possession of the land, through prayer and faith. If we fail to possess our land, then we become disobedient to God.
3. Your land is the promise God has specifically given you (through prophecy, vision or dream or the Bible).
4. We should not be worried about how to possess the land because God has already given it to us. All we have to do is to take a step of faith and act.
5. When we possess the land God wants us to occupy it and bring life to it to the benefits of humanity.
6. There is nothing like a fallow land. If you fail to possess your land, Satan will occupy it and deny you of your blessings.
7. God has performed His part by giving us the land; that is, giving us the power to possess it. It is our duty to possess it now.

Prayer: Train my hands to battle in prayer. Give me divine wisdom to act on every promise concerning my life and my family so that we can possess our blessings. In Jesus' Name. Amen.

What action(s) will I take today to improve my life?

_____
_____
_____
_____

God does not give you big faith, He gives you little faith to enable you grow your faith. It's your responsibility to build your faith strong

Pastor Chris Oyakhilome (How to Make Your Faith Work)

February 28

Be Strong in God

Scripture reading: Ephesians 6:10-20

Ephesians 6:10
Finally, my brethren, be strong in the Lord and in the power of His might.

1. Apostle Paul was giving his last statements in the Book of Ephesians. The last or concluding statements in a man's conversation is very important. Always take it seriously.
2. Although God has given us all the tools we need to live in victory and godliness, we have to play our part by putting them into practice.
3. "Be strong in the Lord"- This is a command; it is not an automatic manifestation. We have to work it out to ensure that we are always strong on the LORD.
4. We can be strong by constantly putting on the full armor of God; emphasis is on "full". Any missing part of the armor can lead to disaster.
5. You put on the full armor of God by constantly studying and meditating on His Word to build your faith; constantly praying in the Holy Spirit (Jude 1:20); and putting the Word into practice.
6. Christians who seek God occasionally are those who fail to put on the whole armor of God.
7. When you make yourself strong in the LORD you will constantly see His mighty power at work in your life.
8. When you make yourself strong in the LORD the devil and his cohorts are no match for you.

Prayer: LORD, You are my strength and my fortress. Without You I have no power. Guide me to always put on the full armor.

What action(s) will I take today to improve my life?

_____

_____

_____

_____

February 29

Your Giving Affects your Unborn Generations

Scripture reading: Psalm 37:21-29

Psalm 37:26
He is ever merciful, and lends. And his descendants are blessed.

1. Being generous and merciful are some attributes of the righteous man.
2. The righteous person is one who has been saved by Christ and continues to live in Him and to live for Him.
3. The righteous man is so blessed such that even in times of hardships he still gives freely.
4. When the righteous lends to people he does not charge any profit (unless it is a profit-making organization) because he understands the benefits of generosity.
5. The righteous sees that continuous generosity is a cyclical means of provoking more blessings. Therefore, he is always seeking for avenues to give.
6. Giving can be made in various forms such as giving of time, money, energy, resources, care and concern. It is about identifying the needs of people and meeting those needs.
7. Giving is one of the ways a man is able to positively affect his generations, even his unborn generations.
8. The blessings of the righteous man cascade to his children's children and those thereafter.
9. The righteous knows that his children and generations unborn will enjoy the benefits of his blessings.

Prayer: Dear God, give me a heart of giving. Let me become a channel of blessings to many.

What action(s) will I take today to improve my life?

_____

_____

_____

_____

March 1

God is Your Father

Scripture reading: 1 Peter 1:13-25

1 Peter 1:17
And if you call on the Father, who without partiality judges according to each one's work, conduct yourselves throughout the time of your stay here in fear.

1. Always make it a habit to call on God, your Father, at all times, for He cares. When you remain silent, He will also remain silent in your life.
2. Some people call on God only in times of need. They use God like a spare tire. This is very insulting to God.
3. Worshiping, praising, thanking God and spending time with Him are also part of calling on Him; it is not only asking for your needs.
4. You are fortunate to have the Everlasting and Great God as your Father. Let Him also know that you are His child by obeying and doing His will. It should be a two-way relationship.
5. God has given everyone a particular work to accomplish on earth. At the end of the day (i.e. when you die) you will give an account to Him. Therefore live your life as one who will give account to God at any time.
6. God is a good Judge. He is never partial. He will judge you according to your heart and deeds.
7. Live your life as a foreigner on earth in terms of not living a worldly life. You can do this by the fear of the LORD because you were bought with a precious price— the blood of Jesus.
8. When you always revere God you are careful to live a holy life.

Prayer: Heavenly Father. I thank You for being a good Judge. Cause me to eternally live for You no matter the situation.

What action(s) will I take today to improve my life?

_____

_____

_____

_____

March 2

You are a King and a Priest

Scripture reading: Revelations 1:1-8

Revelations 1:6
And has made us kings and priests to His God and Father, to Him be glory and dominion forever and ever. Amen.

1. Christ has made us kings and priests to be of service to God.
2. We can only be kings and priests on earth. That is the authority God has given us. Therefore, if you live and do not exert your kingship and priesthood role/influence on earth you are not living up to God's command and you cannot experience His glory.
3. When we take dominion on earth to the glory of God we are serving Him.
4. As a Christian you are a king. You should take dominion everywhere you find yourself. You should be the head and not the tail. You should always be the best wherever you find yourself. For instance, Joseph was a king (in-charge) even in prison.
5. You should not allow the world to rule you, but cause the opposite to happen. You should not allow the devil to influence you but take total dominion over him.
6. You do not need to wait for your pastor when calamity strikes, but take charge of every situation as a priest.
7. As a Christian you are a priest. You should be able to enter into the presence of God, both physically and spiritually, without the assistant of any praise and worship team.
8. You should stand in the gap for your family, friends and your nation. You should intercede for others; offer prayers on their behalf. You should be able to offer sacrifices for your family through service to God.
9. By your priesthood role you must lead people to God through evangelism, prayer, your lifestyle etc.

10. You should teach your children and those under your influence about God and the things of God. Indeed, you are a king and a priest!

Prayer: Thank You Jesus for making me a king and a priest. Train me to exert my godly influence wherever I go.

What action(s) will I take today to improve my life?

_____

_____

_____

_____

March 3

The Forgiveness of God

Scripture reading: Romans 3:21-31

Romans 3:25-26
Whom God set forth as a propitiation by His blood, through faith, to demonstrate His righteousness, because in His forbearance God had passed over the sins that were previously committed, to demonstrate at the present time His righteousness, that He might be just and the justifier of the one who has faith in Jesus.

1. After Christ carried all our sin on the cross God demonstrated His righteousness to us by cancelling our sin. We can, however, experience this forgiveness only if we accept Christ (through faith).
2. Indeed we are justified by faith (not deeds) in God through Jesus Christ.
3. Because of the faith we have in Christ we are free from the bondage of sin and destruction.
4. Justification has made us a righteous people.
5. When we forgive one another we are therefore demonstrating the righteousness of God.
6. Forgiveness entails forbearing one's offense against you and refusing to pay back with evil.
7. Corrie ten Boom said: "God has taken our sin and thrown it into the sea of forgetfulness and posted a sign that says, 'No fishing allowed'".

Prayer: I am forever grateful that You have shown me Your righteousness. LORD help me to also forgive those who wrong me.

What action(s) will I take today to improve my life?

_____
_____
_____
_____

March 4

Have a Good Motive (Heart) in All You Do

Scripture reading: 1 Corinthians 13:1-8

1 Corinthians 13:3
And though I bestow all my goods to feed the poor, and though I give my body to be burned, but have not love, it profits me nothing.

1. Some people pretend to serve or help others with their hearts but in reality they do it for public recognition.
2. Some people seem to do a lot of things in church but their heart is not in it.
3. Some do it for self-glorification; others, for self-gain, money or favor.
4. Others exhibit self-pride in what they do and boast about it. None of these groups of people will have any reward from the LORD.
5. It may be difficult to do things with the right motive until you realize that everything you do is as though it is for the LORD.
6. We only look at things we see but God sees the heart.
7. We should do everything with love as the ultimate motive at all times.
8. Love gives meaning to our sacrifice and makes it genuine.

Prayer: Dear LORD, please let me have a good motive for everything I do that I may receive abundant blessing from You.

What action(s) will I take today to improve my life?

_____

_____

_____

_____

March 5

Become Great through Service

Scripture reading: Mark 10:35-45

Mark 10:43
Yet it shall not be so among you. But whoever desires to become great among you shall be your servant.

1. The best boss or master is one who has been a good servant.
2. The best master exhibits the true character of a servant because of his/her experience with service.
3. The best master always exhibits the character of a servant, so that his/her subordinates will also emulate.
4. Servanthood is the highway to greatness (and high position).
5. Humility is the key to greatness. Someone can be a servant and yet have a proud heart.
6. Greatness can only be earned and bought, sold or given as a gift.
7. Although God has predestined everyone to be great, becoming great is a choice. We must desire for it and also work towards achieving it.
8. To become great is a process (a journey), not a destination. You need patience and humility to get there.

Prayer: Holy Spirit, give me the heart of a servant, a true heart of humility, so that I can learn to become a great leader in Jesus' Name. Amen,

What action(s) will I take today to improve my life?

_____

_____

_____

_____

The best thing a parent can do for a child is to love his/her spouse

Zig Ziglar (See You at the Top)

March 6

Love God and People

Scripture reading: Matthew 22:34-40

Matthew 22:37-39
Jesus said to him, "'You shall love the Lord your God with all your heart, with all your soul, and with all your mind.' This is the first and great commandment. And the second is like it: 'You shall love your neighbor as yourself.'

1. To love God is to obey His commandments, therefore, set your priorities right and let God lead you to love Him.
2. We must love God with our all and all (i.e. heart, soul, mind and body).
3. When you love God you must transfer it to your neighbor, otherwise your love is questionable.
4. When we take people for granted we find it difficult to love them, even without realizing it.
5. If someone says, "I love God," and hates his brother, he is a liar; for he who does not love his brother whom he has seen, how can he love God whom he has not seen? (1 John 4:20)
6. When you have true love the rest of the fruit of the spirit (Galatians 5:22-23) becomes easy to obtain.
7. We are not perfect in loving but when we avail ourselves to God He makes us loving people.
8. When you fail in some aspects of loving God and people, some things can delay in your life.
9. Let your prayer be: "God teach me how to love daily".

Prayer: Let Your love fill my heart daily that it may overflow to those around me.

What action(s) will I take today to improve my life?

_____

_____

_____

_____

March 7

Ask Big Things

Scripture reading: Matthew 7:7-12

Matthew 7:11
If you then, being evil, know how to give good gifts to your children, how much more will your Father who is in heaven give good things to those who ask Him!

1. In regards to the fall of man (Adam) humans are naturally evil. It takes only God through Jesus Christ to make one righteous.
2. No matter how evil one may be he/she wants the best for him/herself or for his/her own. Even Satan wants things that will make him happy.
3. It definitely means that God also wants great things for His own, especially you!
4. If (evil) men who are obviously not omnipotent desire to give good things to their children, how much more will not God, The Omnipotent One, give great stuffs to us, His Children.
5. God is always willing to give gifts to His children. He takes delights in that, however, our requests need to be in His will and also ask Him with a good heart or intention.
6. God takes pleasure when we ask Him things that will give us a comfortable life.
7. When you desire for something you will not get it until you ask. Desire is not enough. Learn how to ask. That is why we need to always be in prayer.
8. Ask big things because you serve a Big Living God.

Prayer: Thank You LORD that You are All powerful and You care for me. In the Name of Jesus, I ask for every big plan [be specific here and ask from Him] you have in store for me. Amen.

What action(s) will I take today to improve my life?

_____

_____

_____

_____

March 8

Stand Firm in the Faith of Christ Jesus

Scripture reading: Matthew 11:1-19

Matthew 11:2-3
And when John had heard in prison about the works of Christ, he sent two of his disciples and said to Him, "Are You the Coming One, or do we look for another?"

1. An explanation to this event could be that John the Baptist may have completed the purpose God gave him on earth— to introduce the Son of God. Probably that is why God did not have to deliver him out of prison.
2. When you reach your peak in life and God starts elevating others, do not be a hindrance.
3. Another school of thought also perceive that God allowed him to be killed due to his unbelief; so that he would not come back to renounce the testimony he made concerning Christ. If you stand in the way of God's purpose, He will take you out.
4. No matter how unpleasant your present situation may be, you should continue to trust and depend on God.
5. When we allow Satan to deceive us in times of troubles he can cause us to doubt God and the situation will begin to overwhelm us.
6. Always be mindful of how you question God or His Word. Do not allow the devil to influence you to speak against God.
7. If you question the Word of God outside of faith, doubt starts rushing into your thoughts and when it is accepted by your heart fear grips you and you begin to believe the devil instead. That is disastrous.
8. When you occupy your mind with God's Word you will not allow thoughts of doubts to settle in.

Prayer: Heavenly Father, help me to never allow difficult situations to cause me to doubt Your potency. Give me the grace to increase in faith during stormy situations.

What action(s) will I take today to improve my life?

_____

_____

_____

_____

March 9

Encourage Others to Christ

Scripture reading: Philippians 3:15-21

Philippians 3:18-19
For many walk, of whom I have told you often, and now tell you even weeping, that they are the enemies of the cross of Christ: whose end is destruction, whose god is their belly, and whose glory is in their shame—who set their mind on earthly things.

1. Perceive God's Word that comes to you as one coming with compassion, purpose and magnitude to save you and give you a greater life.

2. Do not get tired of God's Word no matter how frequent the same Word comes to you. Repetition is the mother of recollection, meditation and learning.

3. The people of the world are enemies of Christ. They despise the power of God and also contaminate the minds of others against the Word of God.

4. As a Christian when you live against the will of God you are living as an enemy of the cross of Christ. You know what is right, and yet refuse to do it.

5. Unfortunately, some Christians allow themselves to be used by Satan as enemies of Christ. They drive people away from the church with their speech, mannerisms and character. Such people will never evangelize.

6. Others may be driving people from the church unintentionally, however, they will also incur the wrath of God.

7. Some people do that for their selfish gains– looking for favor, popularity and satisfaction for their stomachs. They only think of earthly things.

8. Some Christians are unspiritual. They bring up issues of confusion in the church. Thinking they are doing the right thing by "defending the church/religion or God", they eventually bring division to the church which later brings shame to themselves. Their end is destruction unless they repent.

Prayer: Holy Spirit continue to fill me with Your presence so I can walk in Your ways. Make me a channel of leading others to You but not otherwise.

What action(s) will I take today to improve my life?

_____

_____

_____

_____

March 10

Make God Your Priority

Scripture reading: Luke 14:25-35

Luke 14:26
"If anyone comes to Me and does not hate his father and mother, wife and children, brothers and sisters, yes, and his own life also, he cannot be My disciple.

1. You should make God your priority in every aspect of your life and in all that you do.
2. Anytime a significant other is becoming a stumbling block against your relationship with God, you should be wise to choose God.
3. If you do not make God your priority you may try to love God and the world (e.g. money, work etc.) equally, which is never possible. You cannot serve God and man at the same time.
4. When your heart goes for someone or something more than towards God, you must be careful.
5. The use of the word 'hate' by Jesus in this context means that you should not love man or anything more than God. It does not mean you should literally hate them.
6. It also confirms the scripture in Matthew 22: 37-39 "Jesus replied: "'Love the Lord your God with all your heart and with all your soul and with all your mind." This is the first and greatest commandment. And the second is like it: "Love your neighbor as yourself." It means that we cannot love God above any man or anything.
7. As we obey this Word we should also be careful to decipher between God and church. Some people seem to spend great time in church while they do not put their house in order. They claim to love God but have a hostile relationship with others, including their close ones.

Prayer: Teach me how to love You LORD above all others. Let nothing or no one come between the love I have for You. I love You LORD.

What action(s) will I take today to improve my life?

_____

_____

_____

_____

March 11

Die to the Flesh

Scripture reading: John 12:20-26

John 12:24
Most assuredly, I say to you, unless a grain of wheat falls into the ground and dies, it remains alone; but if it dies, it produces much grain.

1. When Jesus uses the phrase "very truly", He is placing great emphasis on it. It is such a profound statement that He does not want us to miss; He wants us to accept it and live by it accordingly.
2. Unless you allow your body/self to "die" and allow your spirit to be alive via the indwelling of the Holy Spirit (through Christ), you cannot be fruitful to God.
3. The initial stage to being fruitful is to give your life to Christ. It is the only way you can "die to the flesh".
4. The second is by the Christian dying to self or to the flesh and allowing the Holy Spirit to always operate in him/her.
5. "Wheat falls to the ground"– you must be down to earth (i.e. humble) towards God and man before you can become productive.
6. When you die in your flesh, as a seed to the ground, you allow the Holy Spirit to feed you with 'nutrients' to make you grow.
7. "To die"– to sacrifice your desires and will for the will of God.
8. Some ways of dying is through fasting and praying and studying the Word of God.
9. It is only when a seed rots and mixes with the soil that it gains roots, produces leaves then later bears fruit.
10. This Scripture is also about evangelism. If you do not talk to others about Christ you become a single Christian. But if you evangelize you become many by adding more people to Christendom.

Prayer: LORD Jesus, this Christian journey is tough for my physical capabilities. Please grant me the grace to continuously submit myself to You.

What action(s) will I take today to improve my life?

_____

_____

_____

_____

March 12

Trials Come to Prepare us for Glory

Scripture reading: Luke 24:13-35

Luke 24:26
Ought not the Christ to have suffered these things and to enter into His glory?

1. Jesus Christ had to suffer in the hands of the Jews and Romans so that we may obtain divine freedom.
2. As Christians, going through difficult times permitted by God is part of the journey. God designs this so He can test us and strengthen us (i.e. our faith); then when we come out successfully He rewards us.
3. No cross, no crown. Glory follows godly sufferings.
4. When we are going through sufferings (permitted by God) we should have a good attitude so that we do not lose hope and miss the glory ahead.
5. We should be mindful not to create troubles for ourselves (by our actions or behaviors) and think it is suffering permitted by God. Useless suffering is unnecessary.
6. In times of troubles we need to exercise patience and endurance in order to hold on to the end.
7. The more we know the Word of God concerning our lives the better we would understand and be encouraged to go through tough times. The promises in His Word will give us courage to forge ahead in the midst of the challenges.

Prayer: Heavenly Father, please give me the courage to go through my trial moments and the grace to continue trusting in You.

What action(s) will I take today to improve my life?

_____

_____

_____

_____

*The battle of life is in the mind and the battle
of the mind is for your focus*

Mike Murdock (Seeds of Wisdom)

March 13

Store Up Good Treasures in Your Heart

Scripture reading: Luke 6:43-45

Luke 6:45
A good man out of the good treasure of his heart brings forth good; and an evil man out of the evil treasure of his heart brings forth evil. For out of the abundance of the heart his mouth speaks.

1. Your personality and character basically grows on the things you feed your mind and heart over a period of time. These things include what we particularly hear and see.
2. Our behavior therefore is always linked to what we have been feeding the mind.
3. These things can either be good or bad and they have the ability to influence and shape our lives.
4. When the mind picks up an idea it gets into the heart by the permission (will) of the person; or most often it is because the person has no defense to resist its influence.
5. When attributes get into the heart they are stored as treasures (for good ones), or baggages (for bad ones).
6. Are you storing up treasures or storing down baggages?
7. We must always cultivate good attitudes so we can bring out good things to edify others.
8. The best way to cultivate good attitude is via the Word of God and avoiding engaging in ungodly conversations.
9. You cannot make yourself a good person. Being a good person is founded on making Jesus Christ as your LORD and personal Savior. Then He gives you the ability to be a good person and live a good life.

Prayer: I express my appreciation for You Jesus for qualifying me to be a good person. Grant me the discipline to store Your Word in my mind and heart. Amen.

What action(s) will I take today to improve my life?

_____

_____

_____

_____

March 14

Let God's Word Cleanse You Daily

Scripture reading: Hebrews 10:19-31

Hebrews 10:22
Let us draw near with a true heart in full assurance of faith, having our hearts sprinkled from an evil conscience and our bodies washed with pure water.

1. God is omniscient. He knows all the intents of your heart. We should always come to Him with a good heart otherwise we deceive ourselves. Pleasing people at the expense of God is fruitless.
2. We are more prone to engage in earthly activities; until we make a conscious effort to constantly draw near to God, we cannot experience Him.
3. It is our responsibility to always draw near to God. It is not automatic neither does it come naturally.
4. One major way to always draw near to God is through daily fellowship or quiet time.
5. Our assurance in Christ becomes more formidable when we allow our faith to increase. As we keep increasing our faith in Christ our assurance in Him is strengthened. We keep increasing our faith in God by drawing near to Him.
6. Assurance and faith are cyclical. One influences the other and they keep on growing if we continue to keep the cycle.
7. The Word of God is like pure water that washes our body, soul and spirit.
8. When the Word washes us it cleanses our heart from guilty conscience.
9. As our body needs to be washed daily, we need to use God's Word to wash our spirit daily— through our daily quiet time.
10. Any time the devil accuses you of a forgiven sin, use the Word of God to cleanse yourself from guilty conscience.

Prayer: Your Word is the cleanser of my spirit, soul and body. I will always walk in it so my faith can never be shaken.

What action(s) will I take today to improve my life?

_____

_____

_____

_____

March 15

Build and Maintain Good Relationships

Scripture reading: 1 Kings 5:1-18

1 Kings 5:10
Then Hiram gave Solomon cedar and cypress logs according to all his desire.

1. Society requires that there is fairness in all human endeavors in order to ensure peace.
2. If you want to acquire something be ready to offer something else which is needful to the other party.
3. Develop negotiation skills so that you can always enjoy win-win situations.
4. If you don't have negotiation skills/ability people will take you for granted and take advantage of you.
5. Whenever you have an agreement/contract with someone make sure you don't break it or tarnish any aspect of it. Be truthful and keep your promises.
6. It is difficult to amend broken trust. It takes a long time to build trust but a moment to tarnish it.
7. Try as much as you can to build and maintain good relationships with people, for you do not know when you will ever need them.
8. When you establish a good relationship with people you get things done easily. Create and maintain your connections.

Prayer: Dear God, give me the wisdom to learn how to live with men. Let me value all my relationships from henceforth. Thank You. In Jesus' Name. Amen.

What action(s) will I take today to improve my life?

_____
_____
_____
_____

March 16

How Do you See God?

Scripture reading: Matthew 16:13-20

Matthew 16:15
He said to them, "But who do you say that I am?"

1. The people in the Bible have described God in many forms, usually according to their relationship with Him and the revelations He showed to them.
2. The question is: how do you see God? What does He mean to you personally?
3. When you have a constant relationship with God, He continues to reveal Himself to you in many ways. Every revelation of Him will be in a higher form which will increase your faith and love for Him.
4. The level of your faith is a function of how you perceive God.
5. Until you define God in your own way your relationship with Him could be shaky.
6. Do not depend on people's description of God. It may not be so real or meaningful to you. Find your own description and you will see that your relationship with Him will constantly be enriched.
7. The way you perceive God usually defines what He becomes in your life or how you further experience Him. Abraham saw Him as Jehovah Jireh, and He provided for him.
8. It is how you interpret your personal encounter with God (usually through difficult situations) that defines how you would describe Him.
9. Many people perceive God as water in a cup, others, as water in a bucket. For some, as a pond; others, as a river and more so, others as the ocean. How do you perceive God?

Prayer: Elohim, You are The Great One. Reveal Yourself to me every time. Cause me to know You for myself for You are my LORD.

What action(s) will I take today to improve my life?

_____

_____

_____

_____

March 17

Always Show Gratitude to God

Scripture reading: Psalm 106:1-5

Psalm 106:1
Praise the Lord! Oh, give thanks to the Lord, for He is good! For His mercy endures forever.

1. Giving thanks to the LORD is the duty of man, for God has always been good to us. At least He has given us life.
2. One way to praise God is through thanksgiving.
3. Giving thanks should be an attitude we always express both in good and bad times.
4. When we give thanks to God we express our gratitude to Him for all He has done for us.
5. When we give God thanks we are also saying we want to see more of His goodness.
6. When we give thanks to God we are also making a mockery of Satan for his disappointed efforts against us.
7. God's love is so great that we cannot help it than to always give Him thanks.
8. We also give thanks to God through our substance, resources and time towards His work and humanity.
9. The love of God is indeed forever; from generations to generations, from eternal to eternal. We cannot measure the end of His love.

Prayer: I praise You Mighty God. You have been so good to me; from my conception You have been merciful to me. Forever LORD, I will proclaim Your name to the nations.

What action(s) will I take today to improve my life?

———————————————————————

———————————————————————

———————————————————————

———————————————————————

March 18

Make the Kingdom of God your Priority

Scripture reading: Luke 11:1-13

Luke 11:2a
So He said to them, "When you pray, say: Our Father in heaven.
Hallowed be Your name.
Your kingdom come.

1. Since the extinction of the Garden of Eden humans have tried to experience God's kingdom in so many ways. Thanks be to God that He allowed Jesus Christ to restore the kingdom to us through His death and resurrection.

2. The kingdom of God is right within you if you are Christian. When you catch this understanding it will be evident in your life.

3. The kingdom of God is: living the life of Christ and doing His will.

4. We can now experience God's kingdom on earth if we accept Christ and walk in His ways. We can experience the kingdom (on earth) by demonstrating the power of Christ in us.

5. It is an error for some Christians to think that they cannot experience God's kingdom on earth, but only experience sufferings. This is Satan's deception to prevent us from enjoying the benefits of God's Kingdom.

6. The main focus of our prayers must be the Kingdom. When His Kingdom is established on earth God's Name is glorified and we experience His reign in our lives.

7. We should indeed enjoy the good things God has designed for us right here on earth. In fact, we make God sad when we fail to experience His goodness on earth. Because that was the main purpose of Christ coming to the world—to establish the Kingdom of God.

Prayer: I am grateful that I can enjoy Your Kingdom right here on earth too. Let me apply the keys of the Kingdom in all my endeavors. In Jesus' Name. Amen.

What action(s) will I take today to improve my life?

_____

_____

_____

_____

March 19

Fresh Word

Scripture reading: Luke 11:1-13

Luke 11:3
Give us day by day our daily bread.

1. God is our Great Provider, however, until you ask Him you cannot experience His provision. Develop an attitude of asking from God, because wishing or desiring is not asking.
2. Develop a daily communication with God through prayer, and the reading the Bible. When you seek God daily asking will automatically be part of you.
3. As much as God gives us daily provision of food He is more able to provide us with all our "impossible" needs.
4. Daily bread for the Christian is not only food and other provisions but ultimately the Word of God. The Word of God produces all our provisions. We should therefore ask God to give us His Word daily.
5. When we come to God, reading His Word, worshipping and being in His presence we should ask Him for His Word for the day or the moment.
6. You need God's Word daily in order to live a victorious life. You need a fresh Word every day.
7. When you starve yourself of God's Word you give Satan chance to meddle in your affairs.
8. A Word can sustain you for a while but it may not be enough to sustain you forever. That is why you need a fresh Word daily.

Prayer: Your Word is a light to my path daily. Let me develop a strong appetite for Your Word every moment.

What action(s) will I take today to improve my life?

_____
_____
_____
_____

Learn to use your emotions to think, not think with your emotions

Robert Kiyosaki (Rich Dad, Poor Dad)

March 20

Jesus is the True Peace of the World

Scripture reading: John 14:15-31

John 14:27
Peace I leave with you, My peace I give to you; not as the world gives do I give to you. Let not your heart be troubled, neither let it be afraid.

1. The disciples and Israelites expected Christ to deliver them from the oppression of the Romans and give them national freedom. However, Jesus left the disciples with His peace which surpasses all kinds of peace.
2. When you have the peace of God you do not live in anxiety and worry despite facing the challenges.
3. When Christ left His peace He left His being with us by the person of the Holy Spirit. He gave us assurance that He is always with us.
4. Christ left His peace to all humanity. However, you must receive it in faith by believing in Him as the Son of God and as your LORD and personal Savior.
5. When you accept Christ the Holy Spirit comes to live in you and then you immediately experience the peace of God.
6. There may be different kinds of "peace" in various forms: money, sex, food, drugs, etc. These kinds of peace come from the world.
7. The world's kind of peace initially looks comforting and attractive but within it lies a dangerous trap to condemnation. The peace of Christ is absolute, perfect and leads to eternal life.

Prayer: I thank You for the peace I experience in You. It gives me assurance that the future is bright. Holy Spirit continue to rule my life so I can enjoy your peace at all times.

What action(s) will I take today to improve my life?

_____

_____

_____

_____

March 21

God is Your Greatest Sustainer

Scripture reading: Isaiah 46:1-13

Isaiah 46:4
Even to your old age, I am He. And even to gray hairs I will carry you!
I have made, and I will bear. Even I will carry, and will deliver you.

1. God wants us to realize His omnipotence. He wants us to always remember that He's everlasting.
2. Whatever God begins He completes. All He requires is your commitment and your faithfulness. In so doing, you and God become a great team to fulfill your destiny and His purpose for your life.
3. God is omniscient. He knows the end from the beginning; He already knows the end even before He begins a matter. That is why you can commit your entire life to Him.
4. God can take care of you right from your conception through childhood, adulthood and old age. Do not be anxious. Do not worry. God is able to take good care of you. He never changes; He is forever the same yesterday, today and forever.
5. God is well able to sustain you through all situations.
6. God knows you so well than anyone else, including how well you think you know yourself. He understands you so well that He can fix that very "thing" in your life.
7. Because God made you He is the best repairer and sustainer of your life. If anything is wrong in your life, He is the best solution. Allow Him to take absolute charge of your life and you will continuously experience His glory (goodness).

Prayer: You are my Helper and my Deliverer. Thank You for securing my future. Amen.

What action(s) will I take today to improve my life?

_____

_____

_____

_____

March 22

Tests Come to Strengthen Us

Scripture reading: 1 Peter 12:12-19

1 Peter 4:12
Beloved, do not think it strange concerning the fiery trial which is to try you, as though some strange thing happened to you.

1. It is not what you really say that matters, but how you say it. When making a submission learn how to win the hearts of your audience by showing humility, respect and concern to them. Irrespective of your status try to identify with them; that is when you can have their absolute attention. Peter addresses his readers as "Beloved or Dear friends".
2. We should always remember that tests are part of our Christian lives and therefore we should not be surprised when they come our way.
3. When you remain surprised in your time of tests events will also take you by surprise.
4. There are many forms of tests, trials and temptations. These may have different connotations depending on the version of Scripture but they do communicate specific meanings.
5. There are tests God brings to us to test our faith. God's motive is to increase and strengthen our faith and eventually promote (reward) us through these tests. A classic example is instructing Abraham to sacrifice his only son, Isaac (Genesis 22:1-19).
6. There are trials or temptations that the enemy brings with the intention to destroy us. God permits them so that eventually His glory will be shown (1 Peter 4:13). Example, the trial of Job (Job 1).
7. There are also trials that we will bring upon ourselves either by our actions or inactions: doing something that is not right or failing to do what is expected of us. For instance, when we sin against God or fail to do His will. Example, Jonah and the big fish (Jonah 1 and 2). Unfortunately, many attribute this kind of

trials to the devil and consequently fail to take necessary steps to overcome it.

8. In all these, we should totally rely on God, stay under His protection and remain faithful to Him. For the ones we allow upon ourselves, we need to ask God for forgiveness, change our hearts, minds and actions, and return to God.

9. Remember, God will never allow any test, trial of temptation that is higher than us to befall us (1 Corinthians 10:13). When He permits it He will definitely give us the strength to endure/overcome it or create a way of escape according to His will.

10. When you seem to be failing in your test/trial/temptation then your strength is small (Proverbs 24:10). Always strengthen yourself in the Lord.

Prayer: LORD, please give me understanding to the situations that come my way. Let me eschew anything that exposes me to self-invited temptations and grant me the grace to victoriously come out of my trials.

What action(s) will I take today to improve my life?

_____

_____

_____

_____

March 23

Christ in You Gives Freedom

Scripture reading : Luke 4:14-21

Luke 4:18
"The Spirit of the Lord is upon Me, because He has anointed Me to preach the gospel to the poor. He has sent Me to heal the brokenhearted. To proclaim liberty to the captives and recovery of sight to the blind. To set at liberty those who are oppressed.

1. In the Old Testament, the Spirit of the LORD was on people but now we have Him dwelling in us. This gives us a lot of privileges and greater power.
2. The Spirit of God lives in us for a purpose, not just for us to enjoy His presence during worship or praises. But to take dominion wherever we find ourselves and establish His Kingdom.
3. He wants us to proclaim the good news, which is Christ Himself. The poor in this Scripture does not refer to those who have deeply rooted financial problems but those who need the gospel.
4. The poorest person on earth is not the refugee who deems one good meal in a week as a miracle but the one who does not know Christ. There are some rich people (with all their possessions) who struggle throughout each night just to have a peaceful sleep/rest because they do not have Christ.
5. The devil has encamped many in bondages and are therefore, prisoners. Sin is a bondage. The cares or worries of life can also imprison us.
6. As we declare the gospel we release such people from bondage.
7. The devil has blind-folded many. We have to employ God's Word to take the scales off their eyes so they can see the light of God and enjoy His liberty.

Prayer: Heavenly Father. I praise You for the anointing. Holy Spirit let me use Your power to liberate others from the bondage of sin and hell.

What action(s) will I take today to improve my life?

_____

_____

_____

_____

March 24

Make Every Moment Your Sabbath with God

Scripture reading: Colossians 2:16-23

Exodus 20:9-11
Six days you shall labor and do all your work, but the seventh day is the Sabbath of the Lord your God. In it you shall do no work; you, nor your son, nor your daughter, nor your male servant, nor your female servant, nor your cattle, nor your stranger who is within your gates. For in six days the Lord made the heavens and the earth, the sea, and all that is in them, and rested the seventh day. Therefore the Lord blessed the Sabbath day and hallowed it.

1. Some people are so religious to the Sabbath and are so enslaved to it. Christ said the Sabbath was made for man, not man for the Sabbath (Mark 2:27). We are not under the law but under grace.
2. The Sabbath was made to serve people, not people to become servants to it.
3. The Sabbath is important for man to rest, reflect on life issues and ultimately make time to commune adequately with his Maker.
4. Jesus wanted the Pharisees to know that He is the LORD of the Sabbath (Mark 2:28) and that we should not bind ourselves with religious laws which does not profit us spiritually. But the Sabbath law was a shadow of the things to come; the reality found in Christ (Colossians 2:17). Many who bind themselves with the law of the Sabbath do so under compulsion. We should serve God from a loving heart, not out of compulsion or under binding laws.
5. It is important to pick a day and duration, and use it as your Sabbath. God regards that.
6. The worse thing is to be busy all week and not have time for God. This is what God hates.
7. Apart from picking a particular day, as a matured Christian, you should observe every day as your Sabbath. Always spend time with God every day in your closet; even if it is 10 minutes.

It's all about constant fellowship with God and the family of Christians.

Prayer: Father, let me not bind myself with laws which can easily shift my focus from receiving Your blessings through grace. Put into me the desire to always seek Your face wherever I find myself.

What action(s) will I take today to improve my life?

_____

_____

_____

_____

March 25

It is Finished!

Scripture reading: John 19:28-37

John 19:30
So when Jesus had received the sour wine, He said, "It is finished!" And bowing His head, He gave up His spirit.

1. The (bitter) drink (vinegar) was the final thing Jesus took to symbolize that all the worse experiences man had and will ever go through was over. It means after He received all the curses of the world He was now ready to die.
2. "It is finished"– Christ finally ended all the tasks God asked Him to perform. He poured out everything that God had deposited in Him before He died.
3. Strive to die empty. At any time in your life, everywhere God takes you ensure that you fulfill all your purposes.
4. "It is finished" also means– no other sacrifice is needed; no other foundation should be laid. We can now build on this solid foundation, who is Christ.
5. Christ has ended every negativity of your life immediately you become His son or daughter. The fact that it may still be persisting does not mean Christ had not taken it away. You have to appropriate your faith correctly in order to experience the full benefits of the cross.
6. After Christ made that statement He humbled (i.e. bowed His head and gave up His Spirit) Himself and died. Humility is very necessary in accomplishing your purpose.
7. Technically, the Roman soldiers did not kill Jesus. Jesus (humbly) died Himself because He is God and no body or nothing can kill Him.

Prayer: Thank You LORD Jesus for being the perfect sacrifice for humanity. I bless You for taking away every curse and shame that was upon me. I'm glad that You ended it all on the cross.

What action(s) will I take today to improve my life?

_____

_____

_____

_____

March 26

Live for Christ

Scripture reading: Galatians 2:11-21

Galatians 2:20
I have been crucified with Christ. It is no longer I who live, but Christ lives in me; and the life which I now live in the flesh I live by faith in the Son of God, who loved me and gave Himself for me.

1. You must always remind yourself that you have been crucified with Christ and also resurrected with Him. This will give you a better meaning/understanding of who you are in Christ so you can appropriate and experience the benefits of the power of His death and resurrection.

2. To be crucified with Christ means: to die to self (the flesh) so that your soul doesn't yield to the desires of the flesh but only to the will of the spirit. That is, you live a spirit-filled life. It means that your body is (literally) dead such that it can't respond (or cannot be sensitive) to worldly pleasures or self-desires. You tune your spiritual antenna so high that it superimposes its influence over the flesh; such that the senses of the flesh are dealt with.

3. If you have been crucified with Christ, then it's no longer your body that lives but the Spirit of God (via Christ through faith) who lives in you.

4. Since you are on earth you obviously live in the body. It is easy for your body to control you. For your spirit to dominate you have to live by the Spirit through faith in Christ.

5. Some Christians are carnal because although they seem to be dead they have not fully committed their fleshly desires to the control of Christ. They allow the desires of the flesh to still reign in their lives.

6. Christ died for us because He first loved us. You need faith to accept His love and live for Him.

7. If you value the love of Christ and how He gave Himself for you, you will be determined to live for Him.

8. When you live for Christ it is not for His benefit. Ultimately you gain it all. You gain eternal life and experience His kingdom on earth.

Prayer: LORD Jesus I commit my whole being to You. I fully submit to You any part of my life that is not under Your control. Let me live for You at all times.

What action(s) will I take today to improve my life?

_____

_____

_____

_____

Great opportunities are not seen with your eyes. They are seen with your mind

Robert Kiyosaki (Rich Dad, Poor Dad)

March 27

Be Attentive to the Voice of God's

Scripture reading: Mark 16:9-20

Mark 16:12-13
After that, He appeared in another form to two of them as they walked and went into the country. And they went and told it to the rest, but they did not believe them either.

1. God appears or speaks to us in diverse forms (implicitly and explicitly) usually using natural forms. However, it is up to us to be in tuned with Him so we can perceive and understand Him.
2. Do not be stereotyped in a particular way you want God to appear to you or want to hear from Him. Sometimes He uses unexpected forms such as strangers or even a wretched person. If you are not spiritually inclined, you will miss Him.
3. How sad will it be if you later realize that you encountered or heard God but did not know? It will be a great opportunity missed.
4. When you are close to God in all your ways you will be attentive to hear Him speak to you at all times.
5. God does not speak to us only when we are in His presence such as in church, prayer time or during our quiet time but more especially during our daily activities. The onus is on us to be attentive to Him at all times.
6. Anytime you have an encounter with God share your experience with others so you can increase their faith and spur them on to establish a deeper relationship with Him.
7. When you encounter God not many people will believe you. Do not be discouraged about their unbelief; continue to declare His goodness. At least someone would believe and be transformed.

Prayer: Heavenly Father, let me be sensitive to Your voice so I do not miss Your ways. Let me talk about the new life You have given me to the world so they will come to the saving knowledge of You. Amen.

What action(s) will I take today to improve my life?

_____

_____

_____

_____

March 28

Rebuke with Caution

Scripture reading: Galatians 6:1-10

Galatians 6:1
Brethren, if a man is overtaken in any trespass, you who are spiritual restore such a one in a spirit of gentleness, considering yourself lest you also be tempted.

1. Although we are humans, we should not allow sin to be part of us. We should make every effort through God's grace to abstain from the influence of sin.
2. We should be our brothers' keeper and help one another to abstain from sin.
3. If you see someone in sin, gently speak to the person to woo him/her (from the influence of sin) towards God. If the person continues to live in sin you still have to be gentle and pray for him/her, because most people in sin are arrogant and would not like to be corrected.
4. Anytime you are rebuking someone living in sin, do it with great caution; out of love, so you do not push the individual away from the saving love of God.
5. When you are helping someone overcome a sin be watchful so that you do not become influenced by that same person. Otherwise he/she could drag you into sin as well.
6. You cannot offer what you do not have. You can help someone out of the bondage of sin if you have built yourself spiritually through the Word of God.
7. If you think you are not spiritually strong to handle someone in sin, you can always find another person like your pastor, church leader or a matured Christian who can handle it better.

Prayer: Build me up LORD in Your Word so that I will be able to help those in sin.

What action(s) will I take today to improve my life?

_____

_____

_____

_____

March 29

Grace is Awesome

Scripture reading: John 1:1-18

John 1:17
For the law was given through Moses, but grace and truth came through Jesus Christ.

1. The Law is God's requirements and expectations for living to mankind.
2. The Law dictates strict regulations that must be abided by man in order to please God.
3. The Law is based on man's effort while grace is based on God's enablement/ability/power (to man).
4. The Law is bondage to man in that it requires man to use his/her own effort to please God. This obviously becomes a burden because man can never please God by his/her effort.
5. Grace is God's ability to man to live an effortless well-fulfilled life.
6. Grace automatically qualifies man into the family of God and gives him the ability to please God with no strive. It gives man the opportunity to live in a relationship with God.
7. Those who live by the Law only do so out of duty. Those who live by grace do it out of love because of the relationship they have with God.
8. The Law is not absolute. It has limitations. Grace is absolute and brings about the truth.
9. The Law is boastful, grace is humble. Those who live by the Law pride themselves in their ability to abide by it. Those who live by grace acknowledge God's power for living.

Prayer: Give me the ability, LORD, to live by Your perfect grace. Let me never depend on my own might which will fail me.

What action(s) will I take today to improve my life?

_____

_____

_____

_____

March 30

Be a Good Listener

Scripture reading: Job 31:29-40

Job 31:35
Oh, that I had one to hear me! Here is my mark. Oh, that the Almighty would answer me. That my Prosecutor had written a book!

1. In times of trouble we need someone to talk to for sympathy, comfort and encouragement.
2. In such times be careful who you share your troubles with. It should be one that you trust and know can give you comfort.
3. The first person to share your problems with is God. He's the only trusted friend who can empathize with us.
4. How can God answer you if you do not communicate with Him? How can you communicate with Him if you don't have a relationship with Him?
5. Make prayer an attitude by praying to God every day, every time and anywhere. By so doing, you will easily go to Him with your troubles.
6. The thought of prayer alone is a demonstration of your faith in God. You pray to Him because you have faith that He will answer.
7. Giving a listening ear alone is able to relieve one from the emotional effects cause by his/her trouble. That is how we show that we care. When the emotional aspect is solved a great deal of the trouble is solved; then the individual now has a clear mind and the strength to think through the solutions to the main problem.
8. Learn how to empathize with people instead of just sympathizing with them. Let them know you share in what they are going through. Pray with them, give them tangible needs that can help solve the problem.
9. No matter what your accusers say or write against you, God has the best hand writing to re-write your case in your favor.

Prayer: LORD Jesus, please help me to develop the culture of bringing all my troubles to you. Let me also be a listener and helper to the hurting.

What action(s) will I take today to improve my life?

_____

_____

_____

_____

March 31

Do it for God!

Scripture reading: Matthew 25:31-46

Matthew 25:35
For I was hungry and you gave Me food. I was thirsty and you gave Me drink. I was a stranger and you took Me in.

1. Generosity is a virtue we all need to practice in our daily lives.
2. We should perceive helping people as a duty (as children of God) and also as an opportunity to enjoy God's blessings on earth and receive great rewards in heaven.
3. Whatever we do to our fellow man we actually do it unto the LORD. Therefore, we should do good so we can experience God's blessings.
4. God has made us conduits of His blessings to people. It is a privilege to avail yourself as God's workmanship (coworker) to be a blessing to others. As conduits of blessings you also experience God's blessings.
5. Many of the simple needs we do not regard is highly cherished by God. These include giving food to the hungry, drink to the thirsty, helping a stranger, clothing people, helping the sick and those in prison.
6. Interestingly there are many things we do not need that are needed by others. Sharing is indeed caring. Your garbage can be someone's gift. Use what you have to get what you need.
7. Since there is blessing in generosity we should not wait for people to come for help. We should identify people's needs and go to them to assist them.

Prayer: Thank you God for revealing that whatever I do for my brother or sister I do for you. Empower me to help people everywhere I find myself.

What action(s) will I take today to improve my life?

_____

_____

_____

_____

April 1

Take Responsibility

Scripture reading: 1 Corinthians 9:24-27

Proverbs 25:28
Whoever has no rule over his own spirit is like a city broken down, without walls.

1. Apart from obtaining the spirit of self-control one has to develop and maintain it through constant practice. God gives the spirit of self-control but it is man's responsibility to utilize this spirit.
2. Sometimes God puts us in a situation where we are forced to develop (learn) self-control. It could be a difficult boss, an annoying sibling or a newly wedded spouse (i.e. when the level of understanding between the two is at the developing stages).
3. Self-control is a defense. It protects one from acting impulsively to situations without carefully considering the consequences.
4. If you don't have control/rule over your life circumstances will control/rule you.
5. The Holy Spirit controls your life only when you submit your spirit under His Authority.
6. Lack of self-control makes you prone to sinful acts such as stealing, gossip, lust and fornication/adultery.
7. Lack of self-control can lead you to develop chronic diseases such as obesity, high blood pressure, diabetes (due to overeating and/or eating unhealthy foods).
8. Lack of self-control can make you so angry which can cause you to act foolishly.

Prayer: Dear LORD, endow me with the spirit of self-control. Teach me to control myself so Your Spirit will always lead me.

What action(s) will I take today to improve my life?

_____

_____

_____

_____

April 2

Tough Times Now, Better Life Ahead

Scripture reading: Mark 10:17-31

Mark 10:29-30
So Jesus answered and said, "Assuredly, I say to you, there is no one who has left house or brothers or sisters or father or mother or wife or children or lands, for My sake and the gospel's, who shall not receive a hundredfold now in this time—houses and brothers and sisters and mothers and children and lands, with persecutions— and in the age to come, eternal life.

1. "Truly I tell you" – God's Word has a definite assurance. It is solid, true and has authority. Whatever He has said concerning your life will surely be fulfilled if you faithfully depend on Him.
2. Christianity entails sacrificing your earthly treasures for heavenly gain.
3. When you become a Christian you must divorce your heart from everything or everyone and let your heart fully go with God; because you cannot serve two masters.
4. Divorcing your heart from (or leaving) your loved ones does not mean hating them. It means you should not allow any loved one to become more important to you than God. Your love for God must supersede that for everyone or anything.
5. Christianity is also leaving (the world and its pleasures) and cleaving (to God with your whole heart).
6. Interestingly we forget that the properties and loved ones are gifts from God. Why should we love creatures more than the Creator?
7. God needs your whole heart; not even 99.9%. He needs 100% of your love and commitment towards Him. This is because if the world gets 0.1% of your heart, it will gradually encroach on the other parts of your heart gradually over time.
8. Any time you stand for God there will be a lot of persecutions (in various forms) from the world. Take heart for God will surely reward you if you stand through.

9. The good news is that when you leave your earthly treasures and follow Christ with your whole heart He gives them back to you in a hundred fold and you also have eternal life. It is like trade one get all free.

Prayer: Let me not give up my faith when things are so hard. Let me love You above all else so nothing come between us. In Jesus' Name! Amen.

What action(s) will I take today to improve my life?

_____
_____
_____
_____

Until you turn at God's reproofs, the Holy Ghost is not permitted to show you the deep things of God

Bishop David Oyedepo (Exploring the Secrets of Success)

April 3

You are Very Special in God's Sight

Scripture reading: 1 Peter 2:4-10

1 Peter 2:9
But you are a chosen generation, a royal priesthood, a holy nation, His own special people, that you may proclaim the praises of Him who called you out of darkness into His marvelous light.

1. You are a chosen people because you believed and responded to God's mercy of allowing His Only Son, Jesus Christ, to die for you.
2. God has selected and made you special among creation, therefore, you should never look down on yourself because He values you.
3. God has made you a priest to intercede for others and present people to Him. As a priest you should speak God's Word to people and draw them close to Him.
4. As a priest you should take the responsibility of your life by committing it to the control of the Holy Spirit. You should not always rely on your pastor. Take charge.
5. God has made you a royal priesthood to express dominion on earth and every aspect of your life. Therefore, do not entertain doubts or thoughts of scarcity.
6. God has made you holy so that you can live a holy life and enjoy the benefits of living for Him. Though you are just one person God has made you into a whole nation. You possess every good thing, including all the resources that pertains to a nation.
7. You belong to God and He has charge over you. You are the apple eye of God. He has the duty to take care and provide for you in order for you to have an enjoyable life. You should be grateful to Him for where He's brought you so far.
8. God has given us all these attributes so we can also do His will.
9. We were once in the world, in darkness and the devil was using us to do his will.

10. When we accepted Christ He gave us His light. Therefore, wherever we find ourselves we should let our light shine.

Prayer: I am glad that You cherish me so much. Thank You for making me Your special possession. Please help me to declare Your light to all people.

What action(s) will I take today to improve my life?

_____

_____

_____

_____

April 4

God's Smiling Face

Scripture reading: Numbers 6:22-27

Numbers 6:25
The Lord make His face shine upon you, and be gracious to you.

1. The greatest thing to happen to you is to experience the shining of God's face upon you.
2. When God's face shines upon you it means He is smiling at/ on you. It means His glory is manifesting in your life. It means you have found favor and grace in His sight.
3. It is important to always bless your household, especially your children. By so doing, you will be establishing a solid life foundation via your words. They will also have success in their daily lives.
4. It is also important to bless anyone who comes your way so that positive-minded people will surround your environment.
5. The blessing from your mouth as a Christian has the power to manifest.
6. The more you speak blessings upon people, you challenge their minds to accept who God has made them and also to accept His promises concerning their lives.
7. When we continue to live in the presence and will of God we will always experience His smiling face in every aspect of our lives.
8. When the LORD is gracious to you, you do not struggle to make things happen.

Prayer: Dear LORD, help me to always to have Your presence wherever I go, so I can always experience Your blessing. Let my words be blessings so everyone around me will be blessed. In Jesus' name I pray.

What action(s) will I take today to improve my life?

_____

_____

_____

_____

April 5

Imitate Christ

Scripture reading: 1 John 1:3-8

1 Corinthians 11:1
Imitate me, just as I also imitate Christ.

1. Jesus is our greatest example we should imitate. In all our ways we should be like Him.
2. God has made us Christ's representative on earth. As we imitate Him we also become examples to others, so that they can imitate Him through us.
3. When we (Christians) exhibit a bad/wrong character people tend to imitate it. It is sad that we give the world the chance to justify the wrong actions they portray due to our "so called Christianity".
4. Some Christians, particularly immature ones, may need a spiritual figure to look up to. They may find it difficult to imitate Christ directly (because they cannot physically see Him) and therefore may need to imitate someone who has matured in Christ.
5. It is not wrong to imitate a Christian who is more matured than you, but let Christ be your ultimate yardstick. This is because man has limitations and may not please God at all times.
6. The danger is to totally imitate someone without relating his/her life to Christ's. You may end up learning the bad characters as well.
7. Your Christian life should get to a level where you can also boldly say that people should imitate you because you imitate Christ.

Prayer: Teach me to imitate You at all times so I can draw others close to You.

What action(s) will I take today to improve my life?

_____
_____
_____

April 6

The Wisdom of God

Scripture reading: James 3:13-18

James 3:17
But the wisdom that is from above is first pure, then peaceable, gentle, willing to yield, full of mercy and good fruits, without partiality and without hypocrisy.

1. There are many kinds of wisdom: wisdom of God, wisdom of men and wisdom of Satan.
2. The wisdom of God is the only one that knows the beginning from the end. Thus, it is the greatest and authentic wisdom.
3. God's wisdom is pure because it has no flaws or uncertainties. It is accurate, dependable, trustworthy, realistic and genuine.
4. God's wisdom brings peace to every situation. When you live by God's wisdom you also become a peace-loving person.
5. When you live by God's wisdom you become considerate of others and show mercy like your Heavenly Father.
6. The wisdom of God teaches you humility and sincerity in life.
7. The wisdom of God makes you a just and an impartial person.
8. The only way you can bear good fruit and fulfill your purpose in life is through the wisdom of God.

Prayer: Thank You LORD for Your wisdom that supersedes all others. I ask that You endow me with Your wisdom in all my ways.

What action(s) will I take today to improve my life?

_____

_____

_____

_____

April 7

Our Strength, Thy Grace

Scripture reading: Psalm 46:1-11

Psalm 46:1
God is our refuge and strength. A very present help in trouble.

1. Until you acknowledge that God is your refuge and strength, you cannot enjoy His divine protection.
2. It is your acknowledgement that shows that you know His protection exists and therefore you can ask for it. "You have received nothing because you do not ask" (John 16:24; James 4:3).
3. God is our refuge because He keeps us under His covering or shelter from the plots of the evil one.
4. Being under God's shelter also depends on you. If you continually stay in His presence His covering will always be upon you. Sin and disobedience can take away God's protection from you.
5. In times of weakness always rely on God for strength.
6. Do not wait to find yourself in trouble before you seek God. Always seek God's strength by staying in His presence.
7. The grace of God enables us to find strength in Him in times of difficulties.
8. God is always ready to help us when we call on Him.

Prayer: You are my strength when I am weak. Keep me in Your presence so I do not miss your refuge. Thank You God. In Jesus' Name. Amen.

What action(s) will I take today to improve my life?

_____

_____

_____

_____

April 8

Give it Up to God

Scripture reading: Philippians 2:1-5

Exodus 38:8
He made the laver of bronze and its base of bronze, from the bronze mirrors of the serving women who assembled at the door of the tabernacle of meeting.

1. We all know that a mirror is a very important accessory to women. They cannot invariably do without it. A mirror is actually part of their beauty; it is a determinant of how they look each time.
2. However, these women who served at the entrance to the tent of meeting decided to give up their bronze mirrors for the making of the bronze basin for the altar of the LORD. They laid aside their beauty for the decoration of God's temple.
3. We should humble ourselves at all times in readiness to give up our precious things or treasures for the work of God's Kingdom on earth.
4. If we become humble to God obedience will not be a struggle; it will be as natural as our daily activities.
5. If you have this mindset that everything you have is given by God, you will not struggle to give back to Him.
6. When God asks you for something, He wants to test your humility and obedience. He wants to know how obedient you are to Him. If you are not fully obedient, He will help you if you seek His assistance.
7. Also, when God asks you for something, He is only giving you an opportunity to bless you more.
8. The test of your obedience to God is a proof of your love towards Him.
9. As you give your precious possessions for God's Kingdom business, He will make you more glorious.

Prayer: LORD You are more precious than bronze, silver and gold. Nothing that I have compares with You. Give me a heart that is willing to give to You and humanity.

What action(s) will I take today to improve my life?

_____

_____

_____

_____

April 9

The Omnipotent God

Scripture reading: 2 Peter 2:4-10

2 Peter 2:9
Then the Lord knows how to deliver the godly out of temptations and to reserve the unjust under punishment for the day of judgment.

1. God, in His omnipotent ability, has demonstrated His power to rescue His own people during times of difficulties.
2. God knows those who are His and knows how to deliver His people from trials and temptations.
3. There is no power in the heavens, on earth, under the earth or anywhere that can prevent God from delivering His people.
4. It is God's responsibility to rescue His people from difficulties; it is your responsibility to live a godly life.
5. All that you have to do is to remain godly in all your ways and you will see the deliverance of the LORD.
6. When you are in a difficult situation and you are downhearted, cast your mind back to the great things God has done for you or someone in the past. Then use that experience as a base to build up your faith.
7. It is not in your power to judge the ungodly. Do not feel angry when the ungodly seems to be prospering. God knows how and when to judge them. Just put your trust in Him.

Prayer: Thank You LORD for Your power of deliverance. Deliver my family and I from every temptation and evil plot of the devil. In Jesus' Name. Amen.

What action(s) will I take today to improve my life?

_____
_____
_____
_____

*To every miracle there is a man-ward side. God requires something
from the one that desires a miracle, and if any man will heed
God's requirements, he certainly will have his miracle*

Bishop David Oyedepo (The Miracle Seed)

April 10

Your Miracle is Right Within You

Scripture reading: Matthew 14:13-21

Matthew 14:16
But Jesus said to them, "They do not need to go away. You give them something to eat."

1. There are so many unnecessarily difficult (or stressful) situations the Christian can experience that are not part of the plans and desire of God. You do not need to go through such.
2. The provision of God for you is not far from you. It is right within you. You can access them if you pray (ask) right, remain in His presence, fully obey His will and perform your part.
3. There may be many alternatives or solutions to a problem in life. But many of such solutions have adverse effects. The best solution is found in Christ Jesus.
4. God has given (entrusted in) you the power as a Christian to change every unpleasant situation you find in your life.
5. God has so much confidence in you, yes you, such that He is given you the ability to rule on earth and over everything that frustrates you in life.
6. Most often instead of weeping and being anxious, God is expecting you to command the situation to your favor because He has given you the creative power.
7. It is sad to remain idle waiting for God's response when He has already given you the ability to possess your desires.
8. Ultimately, God wants you to use the power/ability He has given you to provide the needs for many.

Prayer: Jehovah, I bless You for giving me the creative power to cause things to happen in my favor. Give me the boldness to demonstrate this power You have deposited in me. Amen.

What action(s) will I take today to improve my life?

_____

_____

_____

_____

April 11

Your Thanksgiving is Evangelism

Scripture reading: Luke 2:36-40

Luke 2:38
And coming in that instant she gave thanks to the Lord, and spoke of Him to all those who looked for redemption in Jerusalem.

1. Jesus Christ is God's greatest gift to man. We should accept and receive Him.
2. Some people, including some Christians accept God's gift (i.e. Jesus) but they do not receive Him (Christ)- Dr. Myles Munroe. They are religious and call themselves Christians but they do not live for Him. They do not have a personal relationship with Him. They do not live according to the Spirit.
3. When God does something for you, no matter how little you may perceive it, you must show appreciation with excitement and thanksgiving.
4. When you show appreciation to God you are concurrently testifying about His goodness to others.
5. Your thanksgiving to God is a means of evangelizing Christ to the world.
6. When you give thanks to God you also encourage others to believe and trust Him for their miracle.
7. Your thanksgiving builds up the faith of others. That is why Satan does not want us to have a testimony or even to share it when God gives us one.
8. Your testimony is not about you. It is not about boasting of your achievements or possessions. It is about what God has done through you. God should be the focus of your testimony.

Prayer: I will continually testify of Your goodness. The things You do for me supersedes my expectations. You are indeed trustworthy. Thank You LORD.

What action(s) will I take today to improve my life?

_____

_____

_____

_____

April 12

Tender Loving Care

Scripture reading: 1 Thessalonians 2:1-12

1 Thessalonians 2:7
But we were gentle among you, just as a nursing mother cherishes her own children.

1. Church leaders and pastors should serve the church/congregation with a loving heart/spirit/attitude. This is because they deal directly with people from different backgrounds, experiences and levels of spiritual maturity.
2. If you treat people with love you will invariably win them to your side.
3. One of the fruit of the Spirit is gentleness. Gentleness is a great virtue.
4. Gentleness is "slow, but sure". It enables one to achieve a goal or a desire with certainty.
5. A gentle person takes ample time to plan adequately before he/she embarks on a venture.
6. A good leader is one who identifies with his/her followers and loves and cares for their needs as well.
7. Always let people around you know how much you cherish, value and appreciate them. By so doing, you will obtain the best out of them. They will easily respond to every task you give them.
8. Be gentle when dealing with people because you may not understand them until you draw closer or you experience their situation.
9. Some leaders mistakenly think exercising authority means acting harshly towards their subordinates. Such leaders feel respected when their subordinates act in fear in their presence. Surprisingly, the subordinates are only pleasing them out of hypocrisy.

Prayer: Teach me to cultivate the fruit of gentleness. Let me be a good leader who will have the interest of others at heart.

What action(s) will I take today to improve my life?

_____

_____

_____

_____

April 13

Manna from Heaven

Scripture reading: Exodus 16:4-23

Exodus 16:21
So they gathered it every morning, every man according to his need. And when the sun became hot, it melted.

1. When God starts to bless you, He usually gives you just as much as you need so He can train you to handle big things.
2. Usually when God starts blessing us gradually, we do not value it and we think it is by our own efforts or just happened by chance.
3. It is our sincere gratitude towards God for the "little things" He does for us that brings us greater blessings.
4. Do not be greedy in amassing wealth by using any means (including evil means). Be content with God's blessings and position yourself for more blessings.
5. God wants us to work so He can bless the work of our hands. He does not give His blessing to lazy people.
6. Indeed, God blesses us, but He wants us to be part of working out the blessings. God will give you the manna but you have to go out to gather them.
7. If you do not realize your role as part of the blessings, you may never experience it.
8. When God's hand is not in a venture, it will not stand.

Prayer: Dear LORD, please show me the ways to actively do my part in appropriating Your Word to obtain my blessings. Thank You for giving me my daily blessings.

What action(s) will I take today to improve my life?

_____

_____

_____

_____

April 14

Beware of Satan's Deceptions

Scripture reading: John 16:7-15

2 Corinthians 11:14
And no wonder! For Satan himself transforms himself into an angel of light.

1. The world is trying to find solutions to its numerous problems which include increasing murder rates, relationship and marital problems, divorce, immoral behavior, disobedient children, strange diseases, etc. However, things seem not to be improving.
2. Others offer short-term solutions with long-term problems, which are even worse than the original problem.
3. There are some agents of Satan who deliberately present themselves as godly and caring people to offer solutions but with evil intentions to destroy humanity.
4. With the advent of technology, Satan's agents do not present themselves as fetish priests or sorcerers anymore. They disguise themselves as professional people (including false pastors) in order to be accepted by the society.
5. These agents of the devil have the purpose to deceive others and turn their hearts away from God so that they can eventually drive God's people to hell.
6. The devil tries to present a solution to your problems in order to distract you and turn your focus away from God.
7. You can detect these pretenders by being rooted in the Word of God and comparing their schemes to the Word. The Word of God is the only tool you can use to test all spirits to ascertain whether they belong to God or not (1 John 4:1-3).
8. The more you spend time with God daily, His Spirit will continue to guide you in all things. He will give you discernment to decipher evil intentions from genuine ones.

Prayer: Open my eyes LORD and let me detect the strategies of the evil one so I will not be deceived. Expose the plots of evil men and put them to shame. In Jesus' Name. Amen.

What action(s) will I take today to improve my life?

_____

_____

_____

_____

April 15

Quick to Listen, Act Wisely

Scripture reading: James 1:19-27

James 1:19
So then, my beloved brethren, let every man be swift to hear, slow to speak, slow to wrath.

1. We should try to listen to God's voice before taking any action on what we hear.
2. To hear swiftly is to listen to the details. It is to listen beyond the words being spoken; the spirit and intent behind the words.
3. To speak slowly is to voice out your thoughts after thoroughly analyzing what have been said and trusting God to give you the best response.
4. You do not react to situations, you respond. Reaction, as the law of physics states, is equal and opposite. It is done on impulse and can result in a detrimental outcome. Response is giving the best and appropriate reply.
5. To be slow to anger/wrath is to summon all the control mechanisms within you to regulate your natural human reaction to a situation (so you put across your point without acting foolishly).
6. People will usually give you the sweetest portion of their story in order to win favor or cover their shame at the expense of others. You need to listen attentively before pronouncing judgment.
7. Our prejudices make us judge wrongly even before one finishes a statement.
8. If you exercise patience and listen more, you will not react in an angrily manner.
9. There are 3 keywords in this Scripture: hearing/listening, speaking and anger. Listening determines the last two. If you listen carefully without wrong judgment, you will speak calmly and wisely and you can control your anger.
10. God has given us two ears and one mouth so we can listen more and talk less.

Prayer: I receive wisdom from You LORD to listen attentively, speak wisely and act responsibly.

What action(s) will I take today to improve my life?

_____

_____

_____

_____

April 16

Put the Word of God into Practice

Scripture reading: Psalm 119:1-8

Psalm 119:2
Blessed are those who keep His testimonies; who seek Him with the whole heart!

1. The testimonies of the LORD are His laws and commands to man for successful living. His testimonies are His Words; His Word is His Son, Jesus Christ. When you have His Son, you should have His testimonies.
2. The Word of God is the source of all blessings.
3. Many people keep the Word of God; they know the Word; they speak it and brag about their knowledge of the Word. However, they fail to apply it to their lives and thus keep living in illusion.
4. Many who fail to apply the Word in their lives do not receive it into their hearts. They do not mix it with faith. They only have theoretical knowledge instead of experiential knowledge.
5. It is good to keep the Word of God in you and even better to continually live by it.
6. You can experience the full benefits of the Word of God only by knowing and putting it into constant practice.
7. When you genuinely keep His Word you will desire to seek God with all your heart.
8. The more you know God, the more you realize there is still more about Him that you do not know, which will stimulate your desire to know Him more.

Prayer: LORD Jesus, please let Your Word take precedence in my heart and give the grace to constantly live according to it. Amen.

What action(s) will I take today to improve my life?

_____

_____

_____

_____

Faith is the confidence of things not seen. Faith without works is dead. When you can picture something precisely and in detail in your mind, you can bring in into reality. It takes confidence and work

Kevin Hogan (The Psychology of Persuasion)

April 17

Faith Transforms Little to Great

Scripture reading: John 6:1-15

John 6:8-9
One of His disciples, Andrew, Simon Peter's brother, said to Him, "There is a lad here who has five barley loaves and two small fish, but what are they among so many?"

1. Andrew was shuffling between faith and some sort of doubt. He hoped that something could be done with the five loaves and two fishes. Simultaneously, he also doubted how it could be worked out. Thus, he described the food as being small.
2. Sometimes as Christians we find ourselves in such a dilemma; believing God and still having some form of doubt.
3. Anytime you find yourself in such a dilemma, do not give up. Continue to hope and trust in God until your faith overcomes doubt.
4. All you need is God's Word pertaining to your situation of need. God will work out the 'how' and the 'when'.
5. It is your duty to trust in God's Word. It is God's responsibility to make it happen.
6. Despite Philip's assertion that even 200 denarii would not buy enough bread for the multitude, Andrew demonstrated a level of faith by bringing the little boy with only 5 loaves of bread and 2 fishes. We should be proactive and always look for solutions no matter how small it may be.
7. Do not despise small beginnings. If Andrew had despised the boy's food, there would not have been a miracle.
8. The little boy demonstrated the spirit of giving and sharing, which we should emulate.

Prayer: Thank You LORD that You are a prayer-answering God. Increase my faith in all situations, no matter how bleak it may seem. Amen.

What action(s) will I take today to improve my life?

_____

_____

_____

_____

April 18

A Heart of Gold

Scripture reading: Acts 28:11-16

Acts 28:15
And from there, when the brethren heard about us, they came to meet us as far as Appii Forum and Three Inns. When Paul saw them, he thanked God and took courage.

1. Some phases of life can be so stressful and heart breaking that you wish they would quickly come to an end.
2. When people find themselves in trouble, it is a privilege and a blessing for us to be used by God to comfort them.
3. Look at how fulfilling it is to be one's comforter in times of need. Be a channel of blessing to others.
4. God brings dejected, anxious and discouraged people into our lives for a reason- for us to be a conduit for God to comfort and strengthen them.
5. When someone comforts or encourages you, acknowledge that God brought him/her to your life. Be grateful to them and give God the praise.
6. Simply keeping a smiling face/countenance is enough to encourage and give hope to someone.
7. Show hospitality to those in need. Those who show genuine care and concern have a heart of gold.

Prayer: Let me cultivate a heart of encouragement and strength for the sake of those in need. Use me as a channel to give them hope. In Jesus' Name. Amen.

What action(s) will I take today to improve my life?

_____
_____
_____
_____

April 19

Complaining about Manna

Scripture reading: Numbers 11:1-17

Numbers 11:6
But now our whole being is dried up; there is nothing at all except this manna before our eyes!

1. As humans, we tend to complain about everything God gives us.
2. Naturally, God may overlook it when this happens once in a while. But when it becomes an attitude you incur His wrath.
3. When we grumble against God we provoke His anger; we show our ingratitude, ungratefulness and unfaithfulness.
4. Always give thanks to God even during hard times. This is the best antidote to our natural tendency to grumble.
5. When you take a careful and honest inventory of your life, you can attest to the fact that what God has given you is far bigger than what you previously had.
6. You can also realize that your situation is better. This will give you a cause to thank God at all times.
7. Never compare your present godly situation to your "luxurious" past life. The devil will deceive you to return to your wasteful past life. A free man has a brighter future than a bond slave. Remember, in Christ, your life is in progress.
8. When you focus on your problem you tend to forget about God's faithfulness and all that He has done for you.
9. You have a choice between two pathways. When you focus on your problem, you forget the power of God. When you focus on God, you forget your problems and rely on Him for solutions.

Prayer: Heavenly Father, please take away from me any attitude of complaining. Let me look at the brighter side of life that once I have You in life my future is secured. Amen.

What action(s) will I take today to improve my life?

_____

_____

_____

_____

April 20

Leadership By Example

Scripture reading: John 13:1-17

John 13:14-15
If I then, your Lord and Teacher, have washed your feet, you also ought to wash one another's feet. For I have given you an example, that you should do as I have done to you.

1. The best form of leadership is leading by example. This is when the leader's effective discharge of his or her role encourages subordinates to also dutifully perform their responsibilities.
2. Your followers do the things they see you doing.
3. Leadership is having positive influence over people by demonstrating your vision.
4. One great attribute of a good leader is humility. By humility, one can win the hearts of many and have great influence over them.
5. Leadership is not about being served, but rendering services to people from a kind and humble heart.
6. Jesus is our LORD and Teacher. Yet He came down to the level of the disciples. He is the best example we can employ in learning and teaching others about leadership.
7. It is a command that whatever God has given us, we should teach or share with people, so they can also teach others.

Prayer: Eternal God, please give me a heart of humility to serve others. Let me always realize that the best way to go up is to serve with a genuine heart.

What action(s) will I take today to improve my life?

_____
_____
_____
_____

April 21

Words Have Power

Scripture reading: Exodus 16:11-16

Exodus 16:15
So when the children of Israel saw it, they said to one another, "What is it?" For they did not know what it was. And Moses said to them, "This is the bread which the Lord has given you to eat."

1. God has given man the ability to give names to His creation. Like Adam did, we still discover or invent new things and give names to them. The same applies to the names we give to our children.
2. It is a privilege to be given such a task, so we need to execute it with caution and directions from God.
3. Because we have been given that power, whatever name we give becomes the function of the thing or the person. Life and death are in the power of the tongue (Proverbs 18:21a). Names therefore, have power to give expression to the item or the person.
4. We should not allow our currently difficult situations to influence what we say; else, negative words will proceed from us and continually affect us. An instance is seen in the naming of Jabez. His mother gave him that name, saying, "I gave birth to him in pain" (1 Chronicles 4:9-10).
5. You should always think about the future of your child, item or situation, before naming or making statements.
6. If confused by a situation, patiently seek to gain an understanding of what is unfolding, before making any wrong assumption or statement.
7. Do not complain about anything God gives you regardless of how unpleasant it might seem. God's love for you is too enormous for Him to give you anything that will harm you.

Prayer: I am grateful LORD that You have ordained me with power. Let me always speak words of life to every situation I meet. In Jesus' Name. Amen.

What action(s) will I take today to improve my life?

_____

_____

_____

_____

April 22

Christ is Our Foundation

Scripture reading: 1 Corinthians 3:5-15

1 Corinthians 3:11
For no other foundation can anyone lay than that which is laid, which is Jesus Christ.

1. Christ Jesus Himself has already laid the foundation of Christianity.
2. Anyone who tries to lay a new foundation is a deceiver.
3. We are supposed to continually build on Christ's foundation in order to continue His mission on earth.
4. Because the nature of a building largely depends on its foundation, we must build according to the Architect's instructions.
5. We must therefore build very cautiously so we do not mar the Architect's purpose for the building.
6. If the builder refuses to build according to the Architect's instructions the building will collapse one day.
7. Remember the Architect's instruction is the Word of God and the Architect is Christ Jesus, who is also the Word of God.

Prayer: I thank You Jesus that You have performed the finished work on the cross. I am glad that You are the foundation of my life.

What action(s) will I take today to improve my life?

_____

_____

_____

_____

April 23

God's Word Gives Light

Scripture reading: Psalm 119:97-112

Psalm 119:105
Your word is a lamp to my feet and a light to my path.

1. God's Word teaches us to know every step of our lives and ultimately directs us to our destination.
2. When your life looks gloomy and you do not know where to turn, God's Word will illuminate your path and give you guidance.
3. Until you have a lamp, you cannot have light to illuminate your path. Thus, without a lamp, there can be no light.
4. The lamp is the Word of the God (i.e. the Logos). When you apply it appropriately it becomes light that gives illumination to your situation (i.e. the Rhema).
5. As we consistently spend more time on God's Word with a willing heart, we gain a deeper sense of understanding of His Word. This consequently enables us to appropriate His Word to specific needs of our lives.
6. Remember, the Word of God is Jesus Christ (John 1:1-2). You can therefore, fully appropriate The Word if you have Jesus Christ as your Lord and Savior.
7. Jesus is the light of the world because He is the Word of God that illuminates our paths.

Prayer: Your Word gives me directions and great ideas in life. Teach me to constantly apply it in all my endeavors so I can obtain success.

What action(s) will I take today to improve my life?

_____
_____
_____
_____

Until you turn at God's reproofs, the Holy Ghost is not permitted to show you the deep things of God

Bishop David Oyedepo (Exploring the Secrets of Success)

April 24

God's Faithfulness

Scripture reading: Lamentations 3:19-26

Lamentations 3:22-23
Through the Lord's mercies we are not consumed, because His compassions fail not. They are new every morning. Great is Your faithfulness.

1. The love of God is so great that nothing can defeat or overturn it.
2. "The LORD'S great love" – This means when you make God your Lord you will continually experience His great love.
3. The love of God is great because it is limitless; He is a merciful God. God still demonstrates His love towards us even when we fail to obey Him. Of course, that does not mean we should take His love for granted.
4. God's love makes Him merciful and He still accepts us when we genuinely return to Him from our wicked ways.
5. When we continually abide in God's love (by doing His will) no enemy can consume or overcome us.
6. Irrespective of how bad or bleak your night is, God's mercies/love are new and abundant every morning. It never fails.
7. The mercies or love of God never fails because His faithfulness is great. God is always faithful. Always hope in Him.
8. One major way God showed us His great love is by allowing His only begotten Son, Jesus Christ, to die for our sin so we can be reconnected to God.

Prayer: I praise Your Name God for Your immeasurable mercy. I am blessed that I serve a faithful God. Your faithfulness gives me hope when situations get tough.

What action(s) will I take today to improve my life?

_____

_____

_____

_____

April 25

Boast in the LORD

Scripture reading: James 4:13-17

James 4:14-15
Whereas you do not know what will happen tomorrow. For what is your life? It is even a vapor that appears for a little time and then vanishes away. Instead you ought to say, "If the Lord wills, we shall live and do this or that."

1. We are blessed that our God is omniscient. He knows exactly what will happen tomorrow.
2. We do not own tomorrow. We do not own our lives. We should therefore not boast about our lives.
3. We should rather boast in the LORD about tomorrow because we know that it is in His hands and He has purposed to make it glorious if we continue to abide in Him.
4. When we boast about tomorrow in the LORD, we are saying with confidence and in faith that we trust in God. When we have faith in God, we please Him. When we please Him, He will fulfill our heart desires.
5. When we boast in the LORD, we are also giving our will to Him so that His perfect will can be fulfilled in our lives.
6. Not knowing what will happen tomorrow does not mean we should not plan. It does not mean leaving things to chance and doing nothing about your situation. Remember, Joshua 1:8c says "…and you shall make your way prosperous".
7. It means that you let God give you the wisdom to plan and depend on Him to empower you to execute the plan.
8. Amazingly, if you boast in the LORD He shows you what tomorrow entails; He gives you the wisdom to plan for it; and He gives you the grace (ability) to make it prosperous (Jeremiah 9:24).
9. Without Jesus Christ in your life, you are like a mist that appears for a little while and is no more. If that is the case, your tomorrow is bleak both on earth and in eternity.

Prayer: You are my LORD and my life. You know my beginning from my end. I commit my entire life to You. I will always boast in You.

What action(s) will I take today to improve my life?

_____

_____

_____

_____

April 26

The Hidden Blessings

Scripture reading: Exodus 16:11-16

Exodus 16:14-15
And when the layer of dew lifted, there, on the surface of the wilderness, was a small round substance, as fine as frost on the ground. So when the children of Israel saw it, they said to one another, "What is it?" For they did not know what it was. And Moses said to them, "This is the bread which the Lord has given you to eat."

1. Sometimes when God wants to manifest His blessings in your life, He covers it for a while to see your attitude towards Him. He uses this experience to make you recognize your own attitude so you can improve on it.
2. If you are impatient you will be unable to recognize God's blessings for you. This is because God's blessings usually come in unexpected forms.
3. Many people miss God's blessings because they look packaged in overalls.
4. It is the "waiting period" that shows your maturity in Christianity.
5. If you do not understand something in your Christian journey, allow God to direct you and also seek help from a matured and trustworthy Christian. Do not develop an attitude of indifference and do whatever your feelings dictate.
6. Instead of wasting your time complaining to one another, always seek help so that you can move on.
7. There is always an answer to any question that is baffling you. Seek the right source- the Word of God.
8. God always gives us His Word. We must be willing to receive it.

Prayer: Open my eyes LORD and let me recognize Your blessings no matter how unpromising they may look. You know the best for me. Have Your way LORD. Amen.

What action(s) will I take today to improve my life?

_____

_____

_____

_____

April 27

Seeking God

Scripture reading: Psalm 27:7-14

Psalm 27:8
When You said, "Seek My face," My heart said to You, "Your face, Lord, I will seek."

1. God is always speaking to us through His Word, dreams, visions and life situations. We should be attentive to His Spirit.
2. God wants us to constantly seek His face so that we will always be in His presence and under His protection.
3. To seek God's face means to recognize His Lordship over your life; to depend solely on Him in all situations; and to let Him know that "you can do nothing without Him".
4. Some Christians only seek God in troubled and difficult times. Such people will seek Him and may not find Him (Proverbs 1:28-29).
5. The guaranteed way to constantly seek God's face is to establish a personal relationship with Him through Jesus Christ.
6. A practical way to seek God's face is to have your quiet-time/ Bible (morning) devotion every day.
7. Since establishing and keeping a relationship is fueled by communication, prayer is one common means of seeking God's face.
8. Although seeking God's face should be a daily affair, you can move to another level by periodically seeking Him through fasting and prayer.
9. Since the foundation of seeking God is a personal relationship with Him, it must be done in love.
10. If you truly love God, your heart will always go out to Him and therefore you don't struggle to seek Him. You will always desire or be eager to seek Him every moment, otherwise you feel a void in your spirit.

Prayer: There is no other place like Your presence. In Your presence I receive strength, joy, peace and grace. Cause me to always seek You. Amen.

What action(s) will I take today to improve my life?

_____

_____

_____

_____

April 28

Do not Entertain Sin

Scripture reading: Psalm 32:1-5

Psalm 32:5
I acknowledged my sin to You and my iniquity I have not hidden. I said, "I will confess my transgressions to the Lord," and You forgave the iniquity of my sin. Selah

1. Once we are humans and live on earth we are prone to err or commit sin against God and/or our neighbor. However, this is not an excuse to sin because those born of God do not continue to sin (1 John 3:9).
2. In case you sin, remember the omniscient God has already seen it. The safest and wisest thing to do is to immediately acknowledge and confess it to Him.
3. Acknowledgement and confession of sin at least prompts you to desist from it. If you ignore it (without confession), the tendency of stopping the sin is infinitesimal.
4. Some people may acknowledge their sin but may not want to confess (rather they cover it) probably because they still want to continue to enjoy the pleasure it brings.
5. Therefore, acknowledging a sin is insufficient; you have to confess it to the LORD.
6. The most devastated person is one who knows his sinful behavior but covers it. Such a person is deceiving him/herself and does not open up to seek help.
7. Sometimes you may not realize sin has crept into your life. If you experience some discomfort or heaviness in your spirit, it may be a sign that you are harboring a sin such as an inability to forgive.
8. Confession must be succeeded by repentance; i.e. change of mind and heart, otherwise it is incomplete.
9. When you acknowledge your sin, confess it and ask God to help you change (renew) your mind. Therefore, acknowledgment of sin should lead to confession and repentance.

10. Remember, God gives you the grace (ability) to change your mind, but it's your responsibility to change your mind and actions.

Prayer: Thank You for the grace of forgiveness. Let me not sin against You LORD. Let me not harbor any trace of sin in me.

What action(s) will I take today to improve my life?

_____

_____

_____

_____

April 29

The Language of Whistling

Scripture reading: Zechariah 10:1-8

Zechariah 10:8
I will whistle for them and gather them. For I will redeem them; and they shall increase as they once increased.

1. It is the desire of God to always gather His people and bring them closer to Him.
2. God is always "whistling" to our hearts and minds to draw us closer. He whistles in a sort of intriguingly melodious manner in order to attract our attention.
3. One practical way God whistles to our hearts is through the promptings of the Holy Spirit. It is so soft, small and gentle sound such that if you are not in tune, you may not realize it.
4. Often, we may not hear God's voice as we expect; He may be "whistling". Tune your heart to His still small sound (prompts).
5. Anytime the Christian is about to fall into trouble God prompts him/her in order to bring deliverance. It is your duty to listen to His prompts.
6. Until you train your heart to detect the still small sound (through constant fellowship with Him), you may remain uncertain to His prompts.
7. When we listen and act according to God's "whistle", He will constantly deliver us from calamities.
8. God will increase us on every side if we listen and act according to His promptings.
9. Increase comes after redemption.
10. We can experience increase in a particular aspect of life unless God delivers us from anything the holds us back in that particular department of life.

Prayer: Spirit of the Living God. I may sometimes be stubborn to obey Your still small voice. Please give me a heart of humility to always listen and obey Your promptings, for in that I will increase on every side. Thank You LORD. Amen.

What action(s) will I take today to improve my life?

_____

_____

_____

_____

April 30

Speak Wisely

Scripture reading: Proverbs 10:17-21

Proverbs 10:19
In the multitude of words sin is not lacking. But he who restrains his lips is wise.

1. It costs us nothing to utter words, but the effects of those words can be devastatingly expensive.
2. Once words proceed from your mouth you cannot take them back. Think holistically before you talk.
3. God gave us one mouth, two ears and two eyes so we can listen more, see more but speak less. God expects us to speak after we have listened and observed properly/carefully (but not vice versa).
4. When you talk too much the tendency to sin (err), lie or speak foolishly is very high.
5. When you talk too much it gets to a point you disengage your senses. At this point your talk is not screened/refined by your mind (because you do not allow, for example, your ears or eyes to send information to your mind anymore).
6. Speaking (communication) requires feedback even from yourself. When you talk too much you do not listen to yourself to get a proper feedback.
7. The tongue is a powerful instrument; a two-edged sword. It can bless or curse, heal or harm, soothe or aggravate and deliver or imprison.
8. One way to avoid erring in your talk is to first listen to people attentively for a while before talking.
9. Even the fool is considered a wise person when he keeps quiet.
10. Know when to talk. There are three groups of people we interact with in life; interactions with individuals who are above us; interactions with individuals at our level; and interactions with those below us. In the midst of those above you, do not talk (except only when very necessary); only listen and ask questions

so you can learn wisdom. When you are with your cohorts, you can talk a little and listen more, so you can share as well. In the midst of those below you, you can talk (and do some listening as well) because they look up to you.

Prayer: Omniscient Father. Teach me how, what and when to talk. In my daily dealings, let me speak wisely to the benefit of myself and others. In Jesus' Name. Amen.

What action(s) will I take today to improve my life?

_____

_____

_____

_____

*The measure of a man is not what he does on Sundays,
but rather who he is on Monday through Saturday*

John Mason (An Enemy Called Average)

May 1

Authority to Win Souls

Scripture reading: Matthew 28:16-20

Matthew 28:18-20
And Jesus came and spoke to them, saying, "All authority has been given to Me in heaven and on earth. Go therefore and make disciples of all the nations, baptizing them in the name of the Father and of the Son and of the Holy Spirit, teaching them to observe all things that I have commanded you; and lo, I am with you always, even to the end of the age." Amen.

1. All authority in heaven and on earth has been given to Jesus after His death and resurrection. It was through His sacrifice on the cross for man that made Him qualified.
2. Until you place your life on the altar of sacrifice for God, you will not attain your promise to the fullest.
3. Everyone has a specific kind of sacrifice God requires; ask God to help you identify yours. Another way to call it is your purpose, assignment or calling on earth.
4. God expects us to leave our comfort zones and go into the world to demonstrate His love to people. We demonstrate His love by telling people about the provision of His salvation.
5. Your Christ-like (Christian) life has the power to influence others onto Christ.
6. When God gives you a purpose/vision He gives you the power/ provision to accomplish it.
7. As part of our task to sacrifice our lives unto God, Christ has given us His authority to lead others to His saving grace.
8. Making disciples of all nations means influencing others around wherever you find yourself with the Word of God, which is Christ.
9. It is your responsibility as a Christian to preach to others about Christ. It is a command, not a request.

Prayer: Thank You Oh My Father for giving us Your Son, Jesus, who has given us the authority to win souls and add to the Kingdom. Continue to place this burden on my heart so I draw people to You. Amen.

What action(s) will I take today to improve my life?

_____

_____

_____

_____

May 2

Eternal Gift

Scripture reading: Ephesians 2:1-9

Ephesians 2:8
For by grace you have been saved through faith, and that not of yourselves; it is the gift of God.

1. The ultimate purpose of God's grace is to bring salvation to mankind. All other products of grace cascade from salvation.
2. Although grace abounds we can only appropriate it through faith in Christ Jesus. That is, if we believe in Christ we can enjoy the products of grace.
3. The grace of God is Jesus Christ.
4. If salvation required running a 20,000km marathon, many would not mind to use their last breath to fulfill that requirement because they want to use their own effort. But praise be to God that you do not have to do anything to gain salvation, except to accept Jesus Christ as your Lord and Savior.
5. Believe in Christ Jesus because it was His death and resurrection that brought us grace to become children of God.
6. The products of grace include redemption from the power of Satan and sin, dominion over satanic influence, and relationship (reconciliation) with our Father (God).
7. The grace that God has given us—through Christ Jesus—is a gift. We never worked for it and we can never work to pay it off. We should therefore not boast as if we were saved by our self-righteousness.
8. Because the grace of God is a gift, He commands us to share it with others, so that they may also become His children.
9. Because the grace is a gift, everything God gives you is a product of the grace. Therefore, do not boast about who you are or your possessions or abilities. Rather, boast in the LORD.

Prayer: Jesus, we extol You. We proclaim You are King. We are grateful for this great gift of salvation You have given us. Thank You LORD. Amen.

What action(s) will I take today to improve my life?

_____

_____

_____

_____

May 3

Go Out and Make Impact

Scripture reading: Luke 5:17-31

Luke 5:31
Jesus answered and said to them, "Those who are well have no need of a physician, but those who are sick."

1. Christ came into the world to rescue the unsaved.
2. Christians are expected to go out into the world to preach the gospel so that others will come to the saving knowledge of Christ.
3. We should therefore allow God to work on us daily so we can become matured in order to impact the world. Otherwise, the world may rather influence us.
4. We can allow God to work on us by being humble and submissive to His instructions so he can use us to change the world for His glory.
5. You can only give out something valuable after you have received it. Be filled with God's Word daily so you can receive His Word and share with others.
6. We live in a world that is sick– sick with immorality, ungodliness, wickedness and corruption. God needs us to change the world.
7. If you really fill your spirit so much with the Word of God, you will have no option but to pour it out to others to benefit (because it will be "burning in your bones").
8. Christ has made us solution to the world. He has made us healers, comforters, providers and deliverers onto the world.
9. If we fail to avail ourselves as God's solution to the world, God will not manifest His purpose in their lives– His purpose of saving them from sin and condemnation.
10. Many churches only focus on its members and forget to reach out to the society. God's purpose for the church is not only for fellowship but soul-winning.

Prayer: LORD use me to be a solution to a hurting and dying world. Let me feel the need to preach Your Word to the world. Amen.

What action(s) will I take today to improve my life?

_____

_____

_____

_____

May 4

Develop an Attitude of Thanksgiving

Scripture reading: 1 Corinthians 11:23-34

1 Corinthians 11:24
And when He had given thanks, He broke it and said, "Take, eat; this is My body which is broken for you; do this in remembrance of Me."

1. Giving thanks to God at all times—for situations big or little—should be part of our lives.
2. Although it should be a practice, it should be meaningful—coming from the heart—and not just a routine.
3. Giving thanks indicates that God is our ultimate source of everything we have; that we solely depend on Him.
4. Giving thanks is a simple prayer of conviction that God is in charge of our lives.
5. In giving thanks we infer that God should (continue to) bless what He has given us.
6. Giving thanks is a form of humility; that we don't have any ability but God's grace (ability) giving us the power to possess what we have.
7. When we give thanks, we show our appreciation and gratitude to God's provision.
8. When we give thanks, we indirectly tell God that we want more. In fact, we "energize" Him to do more.
9. When we give thanks publicly we magnify God and show forth His power (handiworks) to the world.

Prayer: You are my Great Provider. You give me all that I need from time to time. I praise Your Name for all You have done for me. Amen.

What action(s) will I take today to improve my life?

_____

_____

_____

_____

May 5

Rise Up against the Storm

Scripture reading: Mark 4:35-41

Mark 4:39
Then He arose and rebuked the wind, and said to the sea, "Peace, be still!" And the wind ceased and there was a great calm.

1. Many a time God allows some difficult situations to happen so that His glory will be seen. If we have this mentality, we will not fret during adverse circumstances.
2. When difficult situations arise God expects us to do something about it. He expects us to exercise our faith by totally involving Him in the situation.
3. Jesus arose and rebuked the wind because the Word of God was in Him. When the Word of God is in you—when you have experiential knowledge of the Word of God—you do not fret or struggle in difficult times, but act based on the specific Word for that particular situation.
4. When Jesus arose and saw the wind it was still fierce until He spoke. Sometimes we demonstrate faith in an incomplete fashion by looking on and not speaking the Word. Faith must be applied to its fullness.
5. The Word will remain dormant in you until you speak or command it. You have power in your mouth as a child of God. Speak the Word and God will act on it.
6. When the great windstorm arose, Jesus also arose against it (to demonstrate that He is greater). Until you arise to engage God in your situation, your problems and challenges will remain the same.
7. When you speak against your adverse situation, you must speak positive things to replace the negative. Otherwise, it can always return. There is no vacuum also in the spiritual world.
8. Every situation requires a specific approach. Therefore, it is important to know the right Word for a particular situation.

When you demonstrate faith to its completeness you will definitely see results.

9. When Jesus said "peace be still", the calmness was far better prior to the one before the storm arose. When you engage the name of Jesus in your situation through faith, it will surely get better.

Prayer: LORD Jesus, when the storms of life arise, teach me to rise above them. Increase my faith daily so I can overcome the storms and enjoy Your peace. Amen.

What action(s) will I take today to improve my life?

_____

_____

_____

_____

May 6

The Great Light

Scripture reading: 2 Corinthians 4:1-12

2 Corinthians 4:6
For it is the God who commanded light to shine out of darkness, who has shone in our hearts to give the light of the knowledge of the glory of God in the face of Jesus Christ.

1. We should always be thankful to God that He commanded His light to shine on our darkness (via salvation) even when we did not know we needed Him.
2. The world does not know it needs salvation because to them there is no better life than what they have. Even those who desire a better life, do not know how/where to obtain it (because they do not know the benefits/blessings of being in Christ). The god of this world (Satan) has blindfolded them.
3. Christians should let their light shine out to the world, so the world will come to the saving knowledge of Christ. We should evangelize The Light so that the world may be saved.
4. The Light that God commanded into our lives is Christ Jesus.
5. God commanded His Light to shine out of our darkness so that the CEO of all darkness, Satan, together with his cohorts (sin, bondage, eternal damnation, etc.) will flee from our lives.
6. Although God has commanded His light to shine in our lives, we should also have a receptive heart to receive it.
7. The Light cannot be comprehended by the human mind. We must receive Him first into our hearts, then He will permeate into every part of our being.
8. Until we allow the Light of God into our hearts through faith, we cannot access the blessing that the Light brings along.
9. The Light of God performs two major functions. The first one is to bring man from eternal death to salvation. The second, which is progressive, is to build the saved man day by day, determined by his/her commitment to God's Word.

10. God's Light comes in the knowledge of His Word that reside in our spirit and mind. The entrance of this Light drives out Satan's deception.

Prayer: Thank You LORD that out of darkness You called me into Your marvelous Light. I pray that you will cause others to experience this same Light through my lifestyle. In Jesus' Name. Amen.

What action(s) will I take today to improve my life?

_____

_____

_____

_____

May 7

Know God for Yourself

Scripture reading: Psalm 62:1-8

Psalm 62:6
He only is my rock and my salvation. He is my defense; I shall not be moved.

1. Make God your (own) Rock and your (own) Salvation, not based on others' experience or declaration.
2. Many Christians make God their reliance/dependence based on only what they have read from the Bible or other people's encounter with God. Know God for yourself.
3. When you know God based on only others' experiences, you will just be making mere declarations with no faith or power backing it.
4. If you are able to say, "The God of ... Abraham, Isaac, Jacob, Moses, David, or even your own pastor", then you should also reach a level of your Christianity, where you can say "The God of [insert your name]".
5. If you can boldly say, "The God of [your own name]", it means Satan has nothing in you and cannot use anything against you. Satan then respects you just as he respected Paul by saying, "Jesus I know, Paul I know, but who are you?" (Acts 19:15).
6. Making God your own stems from a maturing consistent, persistence healthy relationship with Him. That is when you have personal encounters with Him and you begin to know Him for yourself.
7. A consistent, persistent healthy relationship with God is one where the Christian makes God his/her friend. He/she is in constant relationship with Him; does nothing without consulting God; lives by Spirit in order to avoid sin (Galatians 5:16); and always pleases God.
8. When you know God personally, your level of faith and confidence in Him explodes exponentially. That was how David was able to declare, "Truly, God is my Rock..."

9. When God is your Rock, He is your foundation, support and reliance. He holds your life together and you solely depend on Him. You trust Him at all times no matter the situation.
10. God is the source of all your achievements; attribute everything you are or have to Him; acknowledge that without Him you can do nothing.

Prayer: Dear God. Help me to constantly build an intimate relationship with You so I can know You more. Reveal Yourself to me and continue to build my faith in You. In Jesus' Name. Amen.

What action(s) will I take today to improve my life?

_____

_____

_____

_____

The Holy Spirit inside you is the way to cheaply disarm the law of sin and death

Bishop David Oyedepo (Conquering Controlling Powers)

May 8

You are an Overcomer

Scripture reading: John 16:25-33

John 16:33b
In the world you will have tribulation; but be of good cheer, I have overcome the world.

1. The Christian journey is not always going to be smooth. There will be difficult times and it is worth knowing so that you are not taken by surprise.

2. Usually, until some problems come your way you do not see the miraculous power of God. In John 9:1-3, Jesus told his disciples that it is no one's fault for the man to be blind, but that the glory of God should be revealed.

3. You experience the healing power of God, when you have a sickness. You experience the provision of God, when you are in need. You experience the counsel of God when you are at a crossroad of life.

4. Perceive your challenges as God's medium to manifest His power and glory in your life. With this assurance, you will always remain calm in your troubles.

5. The joy is that Jesus Christ has overcome the systems of the world, both physically and spiritually. We should therefore focus on the victory ahead instead of the tribulations we may be going through.

6. Whatever troubles you may be going through, Christ has already experienced them while on earth. That is why He has given you the assurance that you should rejoice no matter the hard times, for He has overcome the world.

7. Remember that: No cross, no crown. No tribulation, no triumph. No trial, no training. Until we go through some of troubles we will not be refined.

8. Even though the devil would like to destroy us through tough times, God's purpose is to strengthen, move us to higher levels

and make us better Christians. Succeeding in such trials also bring glory to the Name of The LORD.

Prayer: I know that tribulations and challenges are part of my Christian life but sometimes I am weak to stand them. Please give me the grace to overcome them for You have made me victorious. In Jesus' Name. Amen.

What action(s) will I take today to improve my life?

_____

_____

_____

_____

May 9

Your God-given Purpose

Scripture reading: Acts 20:22-28

Acts 20:24
But none of these things move me; nor do I count my life dear to myself, so that I may finish my race with joy, and the ministry which I received from the Lord Jesus, to testify to the gospel of the grace of God.

1. Although Paul knew he was going to be imprisoned and go through tribulation for the sake of the gospel, he still went ahead because of the task/purpose God had given him.
2. God has given every one of us a task and a ministry to fulfill while on earth. Our aim is to discover and keep focus to accomplish our purpose.
3. Aside from the specific purpose God has given every Christian, we also have the general task to testify about the gospel (good news) to others, so they come to the saving knowledge/grace of Jesus Christ.
4. Looking beyond the problems and focusing on your God-given task and the reward ahead, can spur you on to overcome the troubles.
5. When you do not allow the troubles to dictate to you but focus on your God-given task, the Holy Spirit will give you the grace to accomplish your purpose.
6. Putting aside your "self" in order to do God's task can enable you successfully accomplish it. Otherwise if you focus on your "self" you will be considering the troubles ahead and abandon the task.
7. Until you consider your life as though it's worth nothing for the fulfillment of God's command, you can neither accomplish His will nor please Him fully.
8. Make God's work your personal work. Make God's purpose your own purpose/passion, and you will not struggle to accomplish it.

9. We should always pray for God's love and the passion towards His work, so that we can always be fueled up to please Him despite the difficult moments.

Prayer: Heavenly Father, please do not let me give up on the purpose You have given me because of the difficulties surrounding me. Give me the grace to finish my race with joy. In Jesus' Name. Amen.

What action(s) will I take today to improve my life?

_____

_____

_____

_____

May 10

Who Do You Seek in Times of Troubles?

Scripture reading: Jonah 1:1-17; 2:1-2

Jonah 2:2
And he said: "I cried out to the Lord because of my affliction and He answered me. 'Out of the belly of Sheol I cried, and You heard my voice'".

1. We all have distressful moments at some point in our lives. During such times that we cannot help ourselves, God can help.
2. We should not wait for difficult times before we seek the LORD. We should seek Him constantly; seek Him while He may be found (Isaiah 55:6).
3. If we seek the LORD only during times of trouble it will gradually reach a time where Satan will make us not even consider God as an option. He will literally cause us to forget God.
4. If you do not already have an intimate relationship with God, how can you hear Him in times of trouble when He speaks?
5. Some people resort to friends, their own abilities, and spiritual mediums (fortune tellers) or other gods in times of trouble.
6. The first option that comes to mind in times of trouble depicts the extent of your relationship with God.
7. Make prayer your first point of call at all times so that God will direct you to the path that you should go.
8. No matter the gravity of your distresses God can give you everlasting solutions.

Prayer: Hear my cry Oh LORD, please listen to my prayer. Let me have an intimate relationship with You at all times. When my heart is overwhelmed lead me to the Rock of Ages to give me strength. Amen.

What action(s) will I take today to improve my life?

_____

_____

_____

_____

May 11

Words of Peace

Scripture reading: Proverbs 15:1-9

Proverbs 15:1
A soft answer turns away wrath, but a harsh word stirs up anger.

1. It is not what you say that matters, necessarily, but how you present or say it.
2. Words are spirit and we should be mindful of the power they carry. Words can build or break someone.
3. The natural man is a reactive being; he reacts to the environment accordingly. If the environment is conducive, he is happy, otherwise he reciprocates the same negative experience.
4. The spiritual man is rather responsive to the environment. He analyses a situation by comparing it to the Word of God before responding to and/or taking a decision.
5. It is the responsibility of the Christian to develop the fruit of the Spirit, which includes patience, in order to respond maturely to situations rather than to react to them.
6. A soft answer is a great weapon that can quench an eruptive anger.
7. When someone expects you to react in an aggressive manner (just as you are being attacked), but you respond with a soft/gentle answer, you cause the person to swallow all the planned insults. In fact, you put the person to shame; you make him/her look stupid.
8. When we choose to respond gently to a harsh statement we bring honor to Jesus and gain respect for ourselves.
9. Likewise, when you speak harshly to someone you elicit anger and may cause the person to react accordingly.

Prayer: LORD Jesus, please give me a heart of patience and a mind of wisdom so I respond to situations rather than react. Let my words bring peace into the lives of people. Amen.

What action(s) will I take today to improve my life?

_____

_____

_____

_____

May 12

Mingle to Win for Christ

Scripture reading: Luke 5:27-32

Luke 5:32
I have not come to call the righteous, but sinners to repentance.

1. Jesus mingled with the believers to build them up, but with unbelievers to lead them to repentance (salvation).
2. The Christian must not be of the world (i.e. living worldly/ungodly lives), but certainly he is in the world. We should interact with the world, not by practicing their deeds, but with the purpose of influencing them unto Christ.
3. Before you can influence or win someone to Christ check yourself that you can withstand their influence also; check your maturity level. Otherwise the world may end up converting you, which will be a disaster.
4. Paul interacted with idol worshippers probably with the purpose of winning them to Christ because he knew he had the maturity to do that without being corrupted (1 Corinthians 8:1-13).
5. Galatians 6:1 says that if someone has sinned, the one who thinks he/she is strong in the faith (spirit) should help the person to come out of the situation.
6. If you think you may fall out of the grace while trying to convert an unbeliever, get a more matured Christian involved. Do not think you are superman by doing it all alone.
7. Anytime you are doing a long term evangelism on an unbeliever always pray for divine wisdom because everyone and every situation is different.
8. God expects you to grow and mature in the faith so that you can become a conduit of salvation for others.
9. You can grow by daily spending time with God's Word and practicing the Word in every area of your life.

Prayer: Build me up to be resistant to the negative influences of the world. Cause me to rather impact them with Your Word. In Jesus' Name. Amen.

What action(s) will I take today to improve my life?

_____

_____

_____

_____

May 13

The Same God

Scripture reading: Hebrews 13:1-8

Hebrews 13:8
Jesus Christ is the same yesterday, today and forever.

1. Jesus is God manifested in the flesh among men. Jesus does not change, He is always the same forevermore; in deed, nature and character.
2. Jesus means "Savior or God is salvation". Christ means "The Anointed One". Having the Savior and the Anointed One in your life is so assuring and refreshing.
3. Everything and everyone in the world is subject to change except Jesus Christ.
4. Because Jesus does not change He is always dependable. He does not say something and changes His mind.
5. We are indeed blessed to have a LORD who does not change His Word or the promises He has given us.
6. Because Jesus is the same we can emulate His lifestyle and learn His ways.
7. You can always entrust all your life to Jesus because He is the only One who is always the same and always sticks to His Word.
8. If you have this scripture (i.e. Hebrews 13:8) in your mind and in your spirit trusting Jesus in good and hard times becomes less difficult.

Prayer: Glory be to God in the highest for giving us a Savior Who is forever the same. Because of that, I can trust in all Your promises. Thank You Jesus. Amen.

What action(s) will I take today to improve my life?

_____
_____
_____
_____

May 14

Jesus, The Light

Scripture reading: Jeremiah 42:1-12

Psalm 27:1a
The LORD is my light and my salvation, whom shall I fear?

1. A light gives illumination, direction and revelation. It enables one to see things hidden in darkness.
2. Jesus Christ is our Light. He overtakes the darkness in our lives. He causes all darkness, including the deceptions of the devil, to disappear from our lives. He causes the plots of Satan to be exposed so we can escape them.
3. The New Testament has given us the opportunity to have a personal relationship with God through the Light.
4. When Jesus lives in you He directs your path.
5. Naturally, man fears darkness and yet finds it difficult to seek for the Light.
6. In order for the Light to be in you, you need to be saved. Until you seek the Light and receive Him you cannot experience Him.
7. When you have the Light He saves you from all darkness, dangers, sickness and poverty.
8. When you have the Light He throws out the spirit of fear from within you, which is the devil's weapon.
9. Christ has given you the power to overcome darkness so that you do not fear anymore.
10. If you do not fear the number one enemy—Satan—then who else will you fear?

Prayer: LORD Jesus, I am excited that You are the Light of the world. Let Your Light shine upon every department of my life so I can exercise authority over every scheme of the devil to experience success on every side. Thank You. Amen.

What action(s) will I take today to improve my life?

_____

_____

_____

_____

Opportunities are missed by most people because it is dressed in overalls and looks like work

Zig Ziglar (See You at the Top)

May 15

God's Treasure

Scripture reading: 2 Corinthians 4:1-12

2 Corinthians 4:7
But we have this treasure in jars of clay to show that this all-surpassing power is from God and not from us.

1. God made man out of clay, filled him with His Spirit and he became a living being. We should therefore be humble in all our ways.
2. God has deposited great treasures in us that we should show forth to the world and bring glory to Him.
3. The treasures God gives us include talents, (physical or spiritual) gifts, potentials and opportunities.
4. God has given treasures to all men; both the godly and ungodly. The fact that the ungodly is using their gifts for ungodly gains does not mean God endorses those acts. It means he/she is misappropriating the purpose of the God's treasure.
5. Since God has given us these great treasures we should not boast with them, but humbly use them for His glory.
6. If any treasure we have is not being used to glorify God, we must redirect our focus and use it to please Him.
7. God will eventually make everyone account for every treasure He has given us. What are you doing with God's treasure within you?

Prayer: How privileged I am that you have made me Your treasure. I feel so special and valuable. I receive grace to effectively use the gifts You have placed within me. Thank You Jesus.

What action(s) will I take today to improve my life?

_____

_____

_____

_____

May 16

God's Love in Action

Scripture reading: Romans 5:1-8

Romans 5:8
But God demonstrates His own love toward us, in that while we were still sinners, Christ died for us.

1. Love is not demonstrated through just empty talk but it is action driven. The evidence of true love is not "in the saying' but "in the doing".
2. Just as faith without works is dead (James 2:26), love without actions is empty.
3. "God's OWN love"- This is the ultimate love God demonstrates to us- by giving Himself (through His Son, Jesus Christ) to the salvation of our souls; we who were once a sinful people.
4. God had to risk His Son because it was not guaranteed that people will automatically accept His salvation after His sacrifice (because He has given man a free will). True love must be exhibited unconditionally to all persons irrespective of them deserving it or not.
5. Because God had to risk His Son, when we (Christians) fail to share God's Word to others (to win sinners to Christ) it saddens His heart because we are making His sacrifice meaningless.
6. Love is demonstrated to those who need it most; the sinners because God showed us His love while we were still living in sin. Unfortunately, those who are still in sin do not realize the need. That is the reason for which we are obliged to share Christ with them.
7. God did not allow us to die in our sins although we deserved to die, but went the extra mile to save us. Because we were sinners God expressed His great love towards us.
8. It is easy to love the loveable; this can be done by anyone. Your love is most genuine when you express it towards those who hurt or hate you. This is an unconditional love.

9. God hates sin but loves the sinner so he/she may come unto repentance.

Prayer: Your loving kindness has brought me towards You. Thank You LORD for delivering me from the bondage of sin and hell. I pray for those who have been blinded by Satan's deception that You may take off the scales for them to see Your tender love. In Jesus' Name. Amen.

What action(s) will I take today to improve my life?

_____

_____

_____

_____

May 17

Forgiveness is Medicine to Your Soul

Scripture reading: Luke 17:1-10

Luke 17:3
Take heed to yourselves. If your brother sins against you, rebuke him; and if he repents, forgive him.

1. The person who can hurt you most is the one who is very close to you; your brother, sister, parent, spouse or best friend.
2. You do not really know how to forgive until you forgive a dear one who badly hurts you.
3. If anybody can just easily hurt you, then check your forgiveness level, ask for the grace of God to learn how to forgive.
4. Some people are so hard on themselves that they cannot even forgive themselves. They still dwell in guilt (due to Satan's deception) on a sin that God had already forgiven them. You cannot forgive others if you do not forgive yourself.
5. Offenses will always come, but it depends on how you handle. If you handle it in a matured way, you will not be affected by it. Conversely, if you allow it to affect you, you harbor bitterness and unforgiveness.
6. When someone sins against you, let him/her know. Many a time people do not realize that their actions has caused any damage.
7. Our level of forgiveness should reach a point where we already forgive people even before they ask for forgiveness. When we do this, we are not really doing them a favor but saving ourselves from harboring hurt, pain, bitterness and self-bondage.

Prayer: Father of forgiveness, please give me the grace to forgive those who hurt me. If I have harbored any unforgiveness in my heart please help me to let it go. Deliver me from any hurt, pain or bitterness. In Jesus' Name. Amen.

What action(s) will I take today to improve my life?

_____

_____

_____

_____

May 18

Seek Help from God in Every Situation

Scripture reading: Psalm 30:1-12

Psalm 30:10
Hear, O LORD, and have mercy on me; LORD, be my helper!

1. The Psalmist referred to God as LORD because he recognizes God as the Master/Owner (of his life) who has the authority over him and the power to change his situation.
2. He also expressed that he has no help from anywhere except God.
3. "O LORD" – The Psalmist expresses humility to God in asking for help. It may also be an expression of the intensity of his agony or need.
4. The LORD here is the Old Testament representation of the futuristic prophecy of Jesus Christ. As a matter of truth The LORD is Jesus Christ.
5. The LORD hears and listens to our prayers. How can He hear if we do not ask? How can He answer if we do not pray (communicate) to Him?
6. Some people wish for help to come their way, but they do not yearn to seek for the help. Wishing is not the same as asking.
7. Others complain a lot about their gloomy situation. They lament about their problems, but do not take it to God in prayer.
8. Recognize that God is your ultimate help. There is nothing too small for Him to ignore and nothing too big that He cannot do.

Prayer: I will lift up my voice every moment to You LORD; for You are my Helper. I refuse to complain or be silent about the challenges that surround me. I will cry out to You always.

What action(s) will I take today to improve my life?

_____

_____

_____

_____

May 19

Involve Christ in Your Daily Activities

Scripture reading: Mark 4:35-41

Mark 4:38
But He was in the stern, asleep on a pillow. And they awoke Him and said to Him, "Teacher, do You not care that we are perishing?"

1. Jesus was in the stern, the deepest (backside) part of the boat, where the effect of the storm (shaking) may be strong, and yet He was deeply asleep.
2. In the midst of our difficult situations if we fully rely on (or trust in) God we will be calm and not be afraid.
3. The disciples relied on their own experiences to prevent the storms from capsizing their boat instead of depending on the Master Jesus who can stop the source of the troubles.
4. Sometimes people use their own thoughts, ideas and strength to work out a difficult situation. Usually they end up struggling for a long time and by the time they realize they could seek God's help the situation may have become worse.
5. When you use your own abilities you only massage the problems; treat the symptoms instead of the disease itself. When we fully depend on God He has the ability to uproot the source and causes of the problems.
6. Inasmuch as God has given us abilities to do things for ourselves we should always recognize His grace upon us and involve Him in our dealings; otherwise we are relying on our own abilities, which can fail at any time.
7. Irrespective of how long you have not sought the LORD, return to Him immediately when the thought comes. It is better to go to Him in a worse condition than to remain in your tragedy, suffering or disgrace.
8. The disciples' queried Jesus in a haughty way instead of asking Him in a humble manner. Some people do not know the appropriate way to ask for help and they end up losing the opportunity to receive it.

9. Yes, God answers prayers. However, until you ask Him He will not intervene. That does not mean He does not care. He has given you the free will to make choices.
10. Jesus cares for you so much and He is only waiting for you to call on Him.

Prayer: LORD Jesus, let me rely on You at all times, including times of trouble. I thank You for being my Helper in times of need. Amen.

What action(s) will I take today to improve my life?

_____

_____

_____

_____

May 20

Kindness is a Virtue

Scripture reading: Genesis 50:15-21

Genesis 50:21
Now therefore, do not be afraid; I will provide for you and your little ones." And he comforted them and spoke kindly to them.

1. We should forgive those who hurt/harm us so we do not harbor the pain and in turn harm ourselves.
2. When we forgive we also have a good relationship with God (Matthew 6:12).
3. When we forgive and show kindness to those who hurt us, we are actually heaping coals of fire upon them (Romans 12:20-21). This would cause them to come to repentance.
4. There are times that the offended may have forgiven you but you still think otherwise and continue to hurt yourself.
5. Sometimes when we forgive others it is nice to make known to them that we have forgiven them so they can have a clear conscience and forgive themselves.
6. Unforgiveness can be a cancer to the soul, spirit and body.
7. Unforgiveness builds walls that only love can break down.
8. Joseph's brothers might have thought he would either kill or imprison them. At least he could have minimized or deprived them from their daily food ration; (since there was famine in the land). But he treated them with kindness.

Prayer: Dear LORD, please let me not repay evil for evil but with good. Let me also love those who harm me and live in peace with all men as Joseph did. In Jesus' Name. Amen.

What action(s) will I take today to improve my life?

_____

_____

_____

_____

May 21

Give it Up and Follow Christ

Scripture reading: Matthew 4:18-22

Matthew 4:19a
Then He said to them, "Follow Me, and I will make you fishers of men."

1. God gave man his free will to make choices or decisions.
2. The greatest decision everyman needs to make is: whether to abide by God's will or his own will (desires).
3. God always calls us to come to the saving knowledge of His dear Son, Jesus Christ.
4. When you heed to the call of God, you must follow His will, otherwise you are still living in your own will (and deceiving yourself).
5. Many people claim they have given their lives to Christ but they are not following Him.
6. To follow Christ is to fully surrender your entire will (life) to Him. That is, every aspect of your life, including your personal and deepest secret(s) life. It means to give up everything/everyone that becomes a hindrance between you and Him. It means to love Him more than anyone/anything else including yourself.
7. When we follow Christ, we imitate Him in every way at all times. It must be a lifestyle.
8. When you obey the call of God He equips you to accomplish specific tasks in His kingdom.
9. In a practical sense, there is no way you can have your own will. Either you surrender it to God or the devil takes it and controls you.

Prayer: In my human nature it is sometimes hard to follow You LORD. Grant me the grace to be used for your glory as I totally surrender myself to you. In Jesus' Name. Amen.

What action(s) will I take today to improve my life?

_____

_____

_____

_____

God's only pain is to be doubted. His only pleasure is to be believed. Until God is believed, He feels no pleasure

Mike Murdock (Seeds of Wisdom)

May 22

Great is Our LORD

Scripture reading: Isaiah 40:21-31

Isaiah 40:26a
Lift up your eyes on high and see who has created these things. Who brings out their host by number?

1. The glory of God is so evident through His creation. Every creation of God (living and nonliving) attests to His wonder and goodness.
2. One thing that makes us not appreciate God's goodness is when we consider creation, processes and situations as naturally occurring events.
3. In fact, you, yes you, are a testimony of God's goodness. Your conception, birth and growing up alone reveal God's wonder, no matter how well science may explain these processes. Clearly, science attempts to explain God's wonder, but certainly God is the author of these things.
4. The fact that a natural phenomenon can be scientifically explained or proven does not mean that God is not the creator of it. The fact that the process of digestion can be explained from ingestion to assimilation and excretion does not mean that God did not create man (as some people claim) to kick start this activity. Remember, since we can scientifically explain how the engine of a vehicle operates to move a car does not mean that the car appeared from nowhere. Even the dumbness person knows it was manufactured by man.
5. We should lift up our eyes unto God at all times. We should solely depend on Him and we will see more of the manifestations of His goodness in our lives.
6. To lift up your eyes also means to take God's Word as it is, believe it and apply it to every facet of your life.
7. It also means that you should focus on God's Word so that you are not distracted by the systems and pressures of this world.

Prayer: Oh LORD my God, how majestic is Your Name above the earth. Oh LORD we praise and magnify Your Name. You are the Pillar that holds everything together.

What action(s) will I take today to improve my life?

_____

_____

_____

_____

May 23

Greater is He

Scripture reading: 1 John 1:1-6

1 John 4:4
You are of God, little children, and have overcome them, because He who is in you is greater than he who is in the world.

1. We are all creatures of God but not everyone is a child of God.
2. Just as being a child to a parent is by birth or adoption, being a child of God is also by birth (i.e. being born again) through faith in Christ Jesus. This is the only way man gets reconnected to God after the fall of Adam (John 14:6).
3. Because we are from God, we are of Him also; just as a child has a lot of genetic characters from the parents.
4. Because our rebirth is spiritual (which is weightier than physical birth) we have the full DNA of God in our being. We can only realize this when we consciously express it (through our thoughts, faith and actions).
5. We are therefore the express image of God and have all the power there is to overcome the evil one.
6. In fact, Christ has already overcome the evil one and has given us that power to put the enemy at his rightful place, i.e. under our feet.
7. Christians are supposed to be on top of every system of the world. We should not be subdued by anything because Christ is greater than anything that is in the world.
8. No matter how huge your situation is, remember that Christ is greater and He has given you the power to overcome it.
9. As much as you allow Christ to be LORD in your life He will always show Himself greater over any enemy that comes your way.

Prayer: I am forever grateful to You LORD that You have overcome this world for me. Let me exercise my authority as a child of the Most High King. Amen.

What action(s) will I take today to improve my life?

_____

_____

_____

_____

May 24

Doing Good

Scripture reading: Hebrews 13:15-25

Hebrews 13:16
But do not forget to do good and to share, for with such sacrifices God is well pleased.

1. Our God is a good God and as such we are also expected to show goodness to others. This is one of the evidences that we are from Him.
2. Doing good should be a lifestyle as Christians, not an option. When we do good we exhibit the love of God to the world, which can in turn draw others to the love of Christ.
3. It is a great joy and blessing to avail ourselves by becoming a channel for God to bless others.
4. Everything that we have has been given by God and is not only for our benefit. We are just custodians of the things we possess.
5. As custodians of God's blessings we are supposed to share with those in need. Until you realize this truth you will always struggle to share with and/or help others.
6. When all is said and done, we will give an account to God concerning everything He has given us.
7. When we share with others we are sacrificing what we have to them. This is what pleases God.
8. To sacrifice your possession to others means to go the extra mile—outside your comfort—and give out the little you have in order to be a blessing to someone.
9. As we sacrifice to others, we are actually sacrificing to God. Every sacrifice we give to God will be rewarded.

Prayer: Dear God, please take away any selfishness and give me a heart of sacrifice towards others. Let me be a conduit of blessing to others through my giving. Amen.

What action(s) will I take today to improve my life?

_____

_____

_____

_____

May 25

Essence of Praise

Scripture reading: Psalm 150:1-6

Psalm 150:1
Praise the LORD! Praise God in His sanctuary; Praise Him in His mighty firmament!

1. Praise is expressing appreciation to God and giving Him thanks for the innumerable things He has done for you.
2. Praise is also thanking God in advance for the things He will do in the future. This is a level of faith that causes you to receive from God at all times. Such a person also converts his/her complaints into praise, trusting God for the great things ahead.
3. Praise should not be an occasional event but the attitude of the Christian. This is because so far as God gives us life we should always give Him praise.
4. When praise becomes an attitude, your walk, countenance, talk and actions will be full of praise.
5. The person who praises God at all times irradiates His glory.
6. The two most important things God has done for us Christians that deserve praise is giving us eternal life and the gift of life.
7. When we praise God we declare His glory and majesty to the world, the devil and his cohorts.
8. Praise has the ability to incapacitate the demonic world so that they cannot execute their evil schemes.
9. Be a walking praise unto God wherever you go.

Prayer: I will praise You LORD at all times. In good times and in bad times, for You are forever the same. Let Your praise continually be on my lips. Praise the LORD!

What action(s) will I take today to improve my life?

_____
_____
_____
_____

May 26

Purpose of Temptation

Scripture reading: 1 Corinthians 4:14-16

1 Corinthians 10:13
No temptation has overtaken you except such as is common to man; but God is faithful, who will not allow you to be tempted beyond what you are able, but with the temptation will also make the way of escape, that you may be able to bear it.

1. God has fashioned man in such a way that no temptation should naturally crush him because He does not bring temptation to destroy us. We are tempted because we are humans. So far as we are on earth we will be tempted.

2. The only time temptation becomes overwhelming is when we do not know God or do not have a good relationship with Him.

3. The temptation will surely come but we should have the mindset that God has allowed it for our promotion.

4. God allows temptation to come our way also to test and strengthen our faith.

5. The temptation of the Christian is purposed for the glory of God to be seen in his/her life.

6. Instead of complaining about your temptation pray to God to give you the strength and the wisdom to go through and overcome it.

7. God is faithful. He will not allow a temptation that is greater than you to come upon you. Those that are greater than you, He delivers you without you even knowing it; like Christ told Peter, "Satan had purposed to sift you like wheat, but I have prayed for you" (Luke 22:31-32). This means that the one that comes your way are those God knows you can handle.

8. God will always provide a way of escape for your temptation depending on your relationship with the Holy Spirit. How can you see the way or hear Him give you directions when you do not have a good relationship with Him?

Prayer: Heavenly Father, endow me with the strength to go through temptations successfully. Cause me to solely depend on You for a way of escape so I do not falter. In Jesus' Name. Amen.

What action(s) will I take today to improve my life?

_____

_____

_____

_____

May 27

Draw Near to God

Scripture reading: Psalm 78:1-20

Psalm 73:28
But it is good for me to draw near to God. I have put my trust in the Lord GOD, that I may declare all Your works.

1. Walking with God is a choice because He has given us our own (free) will. You must consciously and personally make that decision today.
2. God is not in need of anything from us. When we walk with Him it is for our own benefit, not His.
3. Our God is full of goodness. He is the definition of good. We can experience more of His goodness when we get close to Him in all our ways. Indeed, God is good!
4. It is not enough to be with God. It is more importantly to be close to Him; just as you have a different relationship with your acquaintances and close friend(s).
5. Some people seem to be with God but they are not close to Him because of that they do not receive their expectations from God. We should always check from within ourselves and never blame God when things do not go well as expected. God is autocratic; not democratic. God is always right.
6. Man sometimes thinks that the instructions or laws of God is to deny us of having an enjoyable life. On the contrary, God's laws have been fashioned to prevent us from falling into danger, to give us directions and also a successful life.
7. Isn't it amazing that our God is Sovereign? It settles all controversies. You are blessed to be a child of the Most High.
8. God is your refuge. Do not be afraid of any situation or anyone. He can sail you successfully through the toughest situation and preserve you from all the schemes of your enemies.
9. Never hide the good deeds God has done in your life. Broadcast His goodness to the world so they also see it and come to the saving knowledge of Him.

Prayer: Draw me closer to You LORD day by day. Let me be in Your presence wherever I find myself, for You are my God. Amen.

What action(s) will I take today to improve my life?

_____

_____

_____

_____

May 28

Disseminate God's Word

Scripture reading: Deuteronomy 6:4-9

Deuteronomy 6:7
You shall teach them diligently to your children, and shall talk of them when you sit in your house, when you walk by the way, when you lie down, and when you rise up.

1. Christians have the responsibility to teach others about the Word of God, particularly those who are within our environment; home, school, church, workplace, etc.
2. The greatest gift/inheritance you can give a child is to teach him/her the Word of God. It is possible to do this because children have little or no life experiences, they do not know much, however, they have receptive hearts to accept anything delivered to them.
3. Since children are imitators of what they are exposed to we must exhibit a true godly nature at all times; at least for their sake.
4. Although children learn from the attitudes and behaviors of adults, we should make it a conscious effort to actively and diligently teach them God's ways.
5. How can we teach others when we do not know? We have a huge responsibility to study the Word of God so we can deliver to others.
6. Make sharing God's Word a daily routine and a lifestyle. Talk about the Word wherever you find yourself.
7. Talk about the Word... when you sit at home- consciously engage others in sharing God's Word; ... when you walk along the road- in your daily routines;... when you lie down- reflecting on the Word before going to bed;...when you get up- studying the Word (for the day) before you step out for your daily activities. By so doing, you make it a lifestyle.
8. When your speeches and lifestyle is full of God's Word you become a medium to disseminate the Word.

Prayer: Your Word is a priority in my life. Let me develop the attitude to teach others so they will also grow in You. In Jesus' Name. Amen.

What action(s) will I take today to improve my life?

_____

_____

_____

_____

The greatest tragedy in life is not death, but life without a purpose. It is more tragic to be alive and not know why, than to be dead and not know life

Myles Munroe (Rediscovering the Kingdom)

May 29

Wonders of God

Scripture reading: Job 38:1-11

Psalm 71:6
By You I have been upheld from birth. You are He who took me out of my mother's womb. My praise shall be continually of You.

1. The Psalmist believed that even when he was in the womb he depended on God. This means that even when we did not know God He still care for us.
2. Even during your delivery process, irrespective of the available experienced doctors and midwives, God brought you forth. That is why you are alive.
3. If God was able to protect you when you were a fetus how much more will He not watch over you and provide for you as you are grown up.
4. If God preserved you in your mother's womb, why won't you make the decision to trust Him at all times?
5. Yes, God will not physically come to your aid or provide for you (because He is a Spirit), but out of His spiritual providence He provides for us (through the people He brings our way) and gives us life (through the physiological processes He has programmed).
6. Natural processes that science has explained should be perceived as the wonders of God, not as natural occurrences.
7. Learn how to acknowledge God for all the wonderful things He does in your life.
8. When we acknowledge God in all our ways we are praising Him for what He has done and for who He is. Develop the attitude of praising God at all times.
9. No matter how difficult life has become, if you think you have nothing to praise God for, praise Him for the life He has given you. He who has preserved you all these years is well capable of taking care of you.

Prayer: I praise You GOD for you have preserved me all these years. You have provided all that I ever needed. I am safe in Your hands, my Everlasting Father. Amen.

What action(s) will I take today to improve my life?

_____

_____

_____

_____

May 30

Knowing God

Scripture reading: Isaiah 11:1-9

Isaiah 11:9b
For the earth shall be full of the knowledge of the Lord as the waters cover the sea.

1. The knowledge of the LORD is multidimensional. The knowledge of the LORD is knowing that God exists and that He is the Creator and the Ruler of the entire universe and beyond what man has not yet discovered.
2. The knowledge of the LORD is accepting God as your LORD and believing His Word.
3. To accept God as your LORD means to allow Him to be the owner of every part of your life.
4. To believe God's Word is to accept Jesus Christ as your LORD and personal Savior; because the Word of God is Jesus Christ.
5. The knowledge of the LORD goes beyond having logical truths; i.e. just having knowledge about Him. It is having revelation of Him; having experiential knowledge, one that you can personally identify with because you have had an encounter/experience with the LORD.
6. If you want the knowledge of the LORD to fill and overflow your life (as the waters cover the sea) spend time on His Word daily and continually put it into practice.
7. When you have revelation/experiential knowledge of God it gives you deeper understanding and the ability to effectively put His Word into practice.
8. God wants His knowledge to fill the earth so many can accept Him and not perish.
9. The knowledge of the LORD can fill the earth if Christians will show forth the glory of God to the world through their lifestyles. We must let the world see the goodness of God through our lives.

Prayer: Dear Heavenly Father, let me have a deeper revelation of You every time, particularly when I spend time with You. And cause me to share the knowledge of You with others. Amen.

What action(s) will I take today to improve my life?

_____

_____

_____

_____

May 31

Resting in God

Scripture reading: Psalm 91:9-16

Psalm 4:8
I will both lie down in peace, and sleep. For You alone, O Lord, make me dwell in safety.

1. Only God provides us with the greatest security. His security is guaranteed, dependable and assured; it never fails.
2. Peace is not the absence the war or troubles; it is being calm and having trust in God in the midst of the troubles.
3. You can value the peace of God only after you have previously gone through troubles so you can appreciate the difference. This will also equip you to encourage and teach others about the peace of God.
4. When you are experiencing some difficulty in a particular area of life you go through stages as you trust the LORD. First, the problems seem to be persisting although you are praying, believing in God and playing your humanly possible expected role. In the midst of these you still remain calm trusting God that He will intervene. This is the faith-building stage. Then things start getting better, however, it seems to be back and forth; that's the fierce- battling stage. This is when many Christians give up. Rather perceive this stage as one whose prayer is effective; that is why the enemy is fighting back. When later God empowers you to overcome the troubles and grants you total peace and rest, you will be at your resting stage. The difficulty becomes history and you have a testimony to share and teach others to come out from a similar situation.
5. The peace of God is not automatic. You have to consciously make Him your peace by constantly depending on and trusting in Him.
6. You trust and depend on God by studying and meditating on His Word and putting it in to practice.

7. When you have the peace of God He makes you relax in Him irrespective of the difficult times.

Prayer: There is no peace in this world but You. Teach me to be calm and trust in You during difficult times. You are my Prince of Peace. Amen.

What action(s) will I take today to improve my life?

_____

_____

_____

_____

June 1

Growing Progressively in Christ

Scripture reading: 2 Peter 3:10-18

2 Peter 3:18
But grow in the grace and knowledge of our Lord and Savior Jesus Christ. To Him be the glory both now and forever. Amen.

1. The Almighty is a God of progress. He wants us to continually grow in Him and not to be stagnant irrespective of our level of accomplishment.

2. We can grow continually by exhibiting consistent persistence in all our dealings with God. On the contrary, complacency can make you stagnant. This is one of the schemes the devil employs to cause us to miss the glory of God in every facet of our lives.

3. God wants us to grow in the grace and knowledge of His Son Jesus because in Him (Jesus) is the embodiment of all that we need and will ever need.

4. Grace is God's power that gives us the ability to do things that we are naturally unable to accomplish. Knowledge (in Christ) is the conscious acquisition of information and truth.

5. It is not enough to have the grace of God. We need to increase in the knowledge of Christ. Grace and knowledge are cyclical. The more knowledge we acquire of Christ the more avenues we obtain to increase in His grace, which subsequently increases our faith to acquire more knowledge.

6. Experiencing the grace of God is God's duty. Having and growing in knowledge is your duty.

7. One needs to grow in the grace and knowledge of Christ, so as to be able to perceive the schemes and deceptions of the enemy and to constantly overcome him.

8. We can grow in grace and knowledge through consistent reading and practicing of the Word of God and dwelling in Him at all times.

Prayer: LORD Jesus, You are the Truth. I pray that I do not become complacent in the knowledge I have of You. Please give me an insatiable desire to seek more of You every day. Amen.

What action(s) will I take today to improve my life?

_____

_____

_____

_____

June 2

Genuine Love

Scripture reading: 1 Samuel 18:1-4; 23:15-18

1 Samuel 18:3
Then Jonathan and David made a covenant, because he loved him as his own soul.

1. The friendship between David and Jonathan is an epitome of true love.
2. We can genuinely love people only if we love them as ourselves.
3. To love someone as yourself is to love the person as your own soul. Inasmuch as you want to make your soul (i.e. mind, emotion and will) happy, you will also long to make others happy and not hurt them.
4. Due to some unpleasant life experiences some people do not love themselves. Such people need to pray to God and probably undergo some Biblical teachings to be healed from the hurt and pain. Unless you love yourself you cannot love others.
5. True love can be expressed if you have experienced the love of God. It is only God who can teach you how to love genuinely.
6. When you love people as yourself, you will not place yourself above them. You will not be selfish towards them.
7. When you love someone as yourself, you are fulfilling the second most important commandment as Christ stated in Mark 12:31.
8. There are different levels of friendship; acquaintances, colleagues, close friends and best friends. Some friends come into our lives to add to and/or multiply our value; others on the other hand, come to take away and/or reduce the value of our lives. You should therefore be careful in selecting your friends because friends can make you or break you.

Prayer: Heavenly Father, if I have any issue of genuinely loving people, please help me to deal with it. Give me a heart of true love so I can fulfill your commands. Amen.

What action(s) will I take today to improve my life?

_____

_____

_____

_____

June 3

God's Abundant Grace

Scripture reading: 1 Timothy 1:12-17

1 Timothy 1:14
And the grace of our Lord was exceedingly abundant, with faith and love which are in Christ Jesus.

1. The grace of God is so great and abundant to deliver everyone from the power of sin into His righteousness.
2. The grace gives us the ability to become what God has destined us to be and to do things that we are naturally incapable of accomplishing.
3. If you have been saved by the grace of God, that same grace through Jesus Christ is well able to empower you to achieve your purpose in life.
4. Always pray/desire for the grace to be fully poured on you daily. For the grace makes us supernatural beings.
5. Anytime you pray for grace you are telling God that you have no abilities of your own but you are completely dependent on His strength. Praying for grace makes you humble and builds your trust in God.
6. Grace has the ability to positively change and transform your heart and life.
7. The grace of God brings faith and love to the Christian. When God saves you (through grace) the grace gives you the power to develop faith in God and true love for Him and for others.

Prayer: Thank You LORD for Your exceedingly abundant love. By Your grace let me continue to grow in faith and love. I pray for Your grace to reach the many who do not yet know You. In Jesus' Name. Amen.

What action(s) will I take today to improve my life?

_____
_____
_____
_____

June 4

A Principle of Receiving

Scripture reading: John 14:12-21

John 16:24
Until now you have asked nothing in My name. Ask, and you will receive, that your joy may be full.

1. God knows all your worries, troubles, desires and needs. He has the ability to take care of all of them. However, the principle is that until you ask Him He will not do it.
2. God is so willing to fulfill your heart desires. He is only waiting for you to ask in prayer through Jesus Christ.
3. We must pray to God in Jesus' Name. Without His Name our prayer is ineffective. Mentioning Jesus' Name with heart-felt conviction is an expression of faith.
4. Praying in Jesus' Name also means we should pray according to His will/Word.
5. If you fail to pray to God about your unpleasant situation, He will look on and do nothing. The power of God in your life will remain dormant.
6. Use the prayer of faith to activate the power of God in order to receive your desires.
7. Wishful thinking is not prayer. You need to consciously make specific prayers to God. Even if you sometimes pray in your heart, your mind and heart should be focused on Him, instead of daydreaming.
8. Since we know that we need God at all times prayer must become a lifestyle, because without it we cannot communicate with Him.
9. At every stage in our lives, until God fulfills a particular need, our joy may not be complete. Find out that very thing that makes your joy incomplete and present it to God in prayer.
10. God wants us to be joyful all the time. That is why He requires of us to ask Him our heart desires in prayer.

Prayer: Let my heart be filled with the need to pray at all times so I can have a constant communication with you. I pray for ... [mention it to the LORD], that You will cause it to come to pass. In Jesus' Name. Amen.

What action(s) will I take today to improve my life?

_____

_____

_____

_____

Do not go past the mark you aimed for; in victory, learn when to stop

Robert Greene (48 Laws of Power)

June 5

Great Humility

Scripture reading: Philippians 2:5-11

Philippians 2:7
But made Himself of no reputation, taking the form of a bondservant, and coming in the likeness of men.

1. Jesus is the greatest epitome of humility for us. Although He is God He took upon Him the likeness of a man and also allowed Himself to be badly treated by His own creation even onto death.
2. If Jesus, The King of kings, humbled Himself on earth how much more should we humble ourselves towards one another?
3. No matter how high and mighty you think you are you must be humble to God and to everyone.
4. "Jesus made Himself of no reputation"– Although God can enable us to exhibit good character, it is our responsibility to make the decision to be humble.
5. In order to be humble irrespective of your high position you must consider yourself nothing; otherwise, your position will naturally puff you up.
6. One of the ways to remain humble is to consider yourself a servant to God and humanity.
7. Humility is so important because God exalts those who humble themselves and humbles those who exalt themselves (Matthew 23:12).
8. If you struggle with being humble, pray to God to cast out any haughty spirit and give you the spirit of humility and servant-hood.

Prayer: Dear LORD, I present myself to You today. Please take away any haughty attitude within me and give me the heart of humility. In Jesus' Name.

What action(s) will I take today to improve my life?

_____

_____

_____

_____

June 6

God's Indescribable Gift

Scripture reading: 2 Corinthians 9:10-15

2 Corinthians 9:15
Thanks be to God for His indescribable gift!

1. Jesus Christ is the greatest gift from God to mankind. He is therefore, God's indescribable gift.
2. This gift of God is indescribable because it is indefinite to be adequately described or defined. To give your only child (son) as a ransom for the atonement of others' sin is extreme and clearly exhibits God's Agape love towards man. Words cannot fully comprehend this great love.
3. Jesus who was without sin came to bear all our sins and curses so we may become righteous and possess the blessings of God.
4. One of the gifts that God gave the Macedonian church was giving. In spite of their hardship and extreme poverty they gave generously towards the work of God.
5. True and genuine giving is a grace we obtain form God because naturally, we want to remain selfish and not give to help others.
6. We can obtain this grace of giving by first of all accepting God's indescribable gift- Jesus Christ.
7. When we give for a good cause, it is not only the receiver who benefits but the giver as well, because God blesses the giver exceedingly.
8. Amazingly, God also benefits in our giving because the receiver praises and thanks God for our obedience to give, thus magnifying the name of the LORD.

Prayer: Thank You God for giving us such an indescribable gift. Your gift has brought me grace and eternal life and so I can also share with others. Amen.

What action(s) will I take today to improve my life?

_____

_____

_____

_____

June 7

Obedience Leads to Deliverance

Scripture reading: Matthew 2:13-21

Matthew 2:13
Now when they had departed, behold, an angel of the Lord appeared to Joseph in a dream, saying, "Arise, take the young Child and His mother, flee to Egypt, and stay there until I bring you word; for Herod will seek the young Child to destroy Him."

1. The Omniscient God already knows the plots your enemies have against you. If you remain close to Him, He will always reveal the schemes of your enemies.
2. When God entrusts a mission to you He gives you the provision.
3. When God gives you an instruction the timing to follow it is very important; not early, not late, should be right on time.
4. It is important to consistently be with God so you can always hear His instructions for your life. You may not know when He would give you another direction.
5. If Joseph had not obeyed God (by taking Baby Jesus to Egypt on time), Jesus could have been probably killed and there would not have been salvation for all of us.
6. It is God's duty to give you a direction and it is your duty to obey it. You and God work together to bring His purposes to pass.
7. God fulfills His purposes on earth through people like you. Oh what a privilege to avail yourself as an instrument to bring the will of God to pass.
8. Remember Joseph was a man like us. He had the choice not to obey God. Anytime you disobey God you delay one of God's purposes from being fulfilled.

Prayer: How important it is to obey Your Instructions Oh LORD. Please give me a heart that is willing to always do Your will at the right time. Thank You LORD for an obedient heart. In Jesus' Name. Amen.

What action(s) will I take today to improve my life?

_____

_____

_____

_____

June 8

Allow God to Always Lead You

Scripture reading: Psalm 23:1-6

Psalm 23:2
He makes me to lie down in green pastures. He leads me beside the still waters.

1. It is God who has the power to make you a great person. He gives you the opportunity to become that great person.
2. To find pasture for a flock of sheep could be a tough task. To find green pasture could even be an unguaranteed and a herculean task; obtaining such successful venture becomes more of a miracle.
3. Green pastures are the blessings of God, which include divine health, prosperity and peace.
4. Like a flock of sheep in the midst of green pastures, God has surrounded you with His abundant blessings. It is your responsibility to claim these blessings.
5. God shows us the way to the glorious path He has prepared for us. It is incumbent on us to be sensitive to His leadings.
6. Still waters indicate peace and calmness. In spite of the difficult situations God will grant you His peace to go through and come out victorious.
7. For you to experience the still waters you have to allow yourself to be led by the Good Shepard, who is Christ.
8. If you are a Christian and you do not follow the Shepard's leadings, do not expect to lie down in green pastures; else, you are just deceiving yourself.

Prayer: Guide me Oh Thou Great Jehovah to go through life's journey. I humble myself to be guided by Your Holy Spirit in all my ways. Amen.

What action(s) will I take today to improve my life?

_____

_____

_____

_____

June 9

A Step of Faith

Scripture reading: Joshua 3:9-17

Joshua 3:14
So it was, when the people set out from their camp to cross over the Jordan, with the priests bearing the ark of the covenant before the people.

1. Joshua who was God's representative to the Israelites already perceived how the Jordan River was going to be crossed because he had spent time with God.
2. When miracles happen in our lives they are the manifestations of God's plans and promises for our lives.
3. The Ark of the Covenant represents the presence and the power of God. Be in tuned with His presence everywhere you go and you will experience His victory upon your life.
4. Do not rely on your own ability. Do not hasten to accomplish your desires. Let God go ahead of you and He will grant you success.
5. Until the priests stepped into the edge of the Jordan it did not depart. Sometimes the commandments of God do not make sense to the mind. He uses it to test the level of our obedience and trains us to trust in Him regardless of the difficult situation.
6. Some Christians want to see some evidence of God's promises before obeying His commands. It does not work that way.
7. God wants you to take a step of faith by obeying His commands so that you will see the manifestation of His promise.
8. When we receive the Word of God it remains dormant until we act according to what it says.
9. Your part is to take the initiative and God will fulfill His part of the promise.

Prayer: Dear LORD. Even when everything seems difficult let me not doubt the potency of Your commands. Build up my faith so I can take the step of faith to realize my miracles. In Jesus' Name.

What action(s) will I take today to improve my life?

_____

_____

_____

_____

June 10

Consistent Persistence

Scripture reading: 2 Timothy 3:10-17

2 Timothy 3:14
But you must continue in the things which you have learned and been assured of, knowing from whom you have learned them.

1. Consistency is very essential in our daily activities, particularly in our walk with God.
2. Many people begin the Christian journey with a lot of zeal but are unable to continue because they lack consistency.
3. Consistency is one of the important distinguishing factors in the end results among people who are able to successfully complete a mission versus those who are unable to complete. The end of a matter is better than its beginning (Ecclesiastes 7:8).
4. One assuring way to remain consistent in accomplishing your plans and purposes is by doing them every day.
5. Study the Bible every day, be committed in doing what the Word says, pray every day, establish a daily deeper relationship with God and you will experience a prosperous life. This is one of the greatest secrets of the Christian journey.
6. You must consciously learn the Word of God in order for it to gain grounds in your mind and heart. This will in turn enable you to live victoriously.
7. To be assured of God's Word is to believe it by faith and be convinced of what it says. Therefore we are admonished to continue in what we believe.
8. In order for people to believe the Word of God you speak to them, they must trust (believe) you also. Your lifestyle is therefore paramount.
9. People will effectively listen to your testimony about Christ when they know you are living the Christ-like life.

Prayer: It will be disastrous for me to fall off the path, LORD. Please grant me the grace to be consistent in my relationship with you. Give me the finishing power to fulfill your will concerning my life. Thank You Jesus. Amen.

What action(s) will I take today to improve my life?

_____

_____

_____

_____

June 11

Never Leave God's Presence

Scripture reading: Genesis 3:1-10

Genesis 3:9
Then the Lord God called to Adam and said to him, "Where are you?"

1. God is always calling those who are lost so they can come to the saving knowledge of His dear Son, Jesus Christ. His desire is that no one is lost (2 Peter 3:9).
2. No matter how far you have gone away from God, He is always ready to receive you by the redemptive power (of the blood) of Jesus Christ.
3. As a Christian if you are not fulfilling the specific purpose/task/assignment that God has given you, then you are outside His will. God is calling you to get back on track.
4. It was not because God could not find Adam but He asked that question so Adam will realize that he has spiritually lost God's presence.
5. Some people think going to church guarantees a relationship with God. They fail to recognize that they can be in church and yet be out of God's presence; because they have not totally committed their hearts to Christ.
6. There are some Christians who having heard God's voice to do His work keep running away from their purpose. Until you take up God's purpose concerning your life you will be going in circles and not experience the full blessings of the LORD.
7. God posed the question to Adam, not Eve, because He had put him in charge. You will account for anything God has put in your possession irrespective of the nature and level of bad influences distracting you.

Prayer: I do not want to leave Your presence dear LORD. Your presence is the sustainer of my life. Enable me to abide in You always no matter the deceptions of the evil one. In Jesus' Amen.

What action(s) will I take today to improve my life?

_____

_____

_____

_____

It is more valuable to seek God's presence than to seek His presents

John Mason (An Enemy Called Average)

June 12

The Importance of Praising God

Scripture reading: Psalm 96:1-13

Psalm 96:2
Sing to the Lord, bless His name. Proclaim the good news of His salvation from day to day.

1. Singing to God every time is part of our worship to Him. We can also sing to God in our hearts (Ephesians 5:19).
2. We praise the Name of the LORD for the things He has done for us.
3. There are so many names and gods that want to be compared to the Name of the LORD. When praising God we should make His Name known to the world that He is the King of all kings and LORD of all lords.
4. A simple but effective way to praise God and make Him known is through our daily conversations with others.
5. When we praise God, we make known His love, goodness, power and handiworks to the world.
6. When we praise God we create an atmosphere for others to believe Him and come to the saving knowledge of Jesus Christ.
7. When we praise God to other Christians we strengthen their faith so they can also believe God to reveal Himself in their lives.
8. When you acknowledge the life God grants you every morning you will indeed sing and make praises to Him day after day.
9. When you begin to count your blessings one by one you will have tons of reasons to praise God.

Prayer: I praise and bless Your Name Jehovah for You are the only God who lives forever. Your Name be praised among all the nations. You are Awesome.

What action(s) will I take today to improve my life?

_____

_____

_____

_____

June 13

Anxiety is Sin

Scripture reading: Philippians 4:4-13

Philippians 4:6
Be anxious for nothing, but in everything by prayer and supplication, with thanksgiving, let your requests be made known to God.

1. God commands us not to be anxious. Paul is not pleading with us. It is a command.
2. Avoiding anxiety is a command because it takes a toll on our Christian lives.
3. Anxiety is tantamount to sin in that it has a destructive ability on your soul just like any other sin.
4. The effects of anxiety are so profound. It affects us physically, psychologically, socially and spiritually.
5. Anxiety is one of the tools Satan uses against Christians. Anxiety makes you worry about a situation so much that you begin to doubt God's ability to help you out.
6. Anxiety has the ability to gradually "eat up" your level of faith and eventually "kill" it if not checked.
7. Just as the enemy came and sowed weeds/tares among the wheat in Matthew 13:25, so does Satan sows anxiety in our faith if we go to sleep (i.e. if we allow him in or do not pray).
8. Anxiety and faith are "antagonistic cohabitants" in the life of many Christians. As the percentage of faith increases, that of anxiety diminishes and vice versa. Learn how to maintain 0% anxiety and 100% faith.
9. The antidote to anxiety is prayer (i.e. communication) to God. Whatever the overwhelming situation may be, present your concerns to God in prayer.
10. Giving thanks to God in all situations drives away anxiety and enables you to trust Him for help.

Prayer: Today, I have known that entertaining anxiety is sinful. I cast out any form of doubt and anxiety from my life and take on the power of faith. In Jesus' Name. Amen.

What action(s) will I take today to improve my life?

_____

_____

_____

_____

June 14

Antagonists to Your Destiny

Scripture reading: Luke 22:39-51

Luke 22:51
But Jesus answered and said, "Permit even this." And He touched his ear and healed him.

1. Jesus was calm during His arrest because He knew that it was part of His purpose on earth but His disciples did not understand at that time.
2. When you are in your purpose and misfortunes happen, do not panic because you will later understand that it is part of the process to your destination.
3. A man of purpose knows that even his enemies (despite the maltreatments and attacks) are propellers to his destiny.
4. Although the disciples thought they were defending their Master they did not realize they were rather preventing Him from fulfilling His purpose.
5. In your distressful moments continue to be good to your enemies; for you will be heaping coals of fire on their heads (Romans 12:20). God will also reward you for your kind heart.
6. When the enemy attacks do not fight by your own strength. Present it to God in prayer and let Him fight for battles. Vengeance is the LORD's (Romans 12:19).
7. The moment you fight back by paying evil for evil or verbal exchange you are telling God you can fight your own battle. God withdraws from you and you are on your own.

Prayer: I do understand that on my way to fulfilling Your plans for my life, enemies will arise against me. LORD, please give me the strength and calmness to endure and overcome such distracting acts so I can reach my destination. In Jesus' Name. Amen.

What action(s) will I take today to improve my life?

_____

_____

_____

_____

June 15

Do Good to People

Scripture reading: Galatians 6:1-10

Galatians 6:10
Therefore, as we have opportunity, let us do good to all, especially to those who are of the household of faith.

1. Doing good or giving is an opportunity that we should be looking forward to.
2. Doing good is an opportunity because it creates an avenue for the giver to be blessed. We should be delighted to look for these opportunities to bless people.
3. Everything you have is given to you by God. He has made you a steward so you can bless others with it. If you consider this truth you will not hesitate to do good or you will never give grudgingly.
4. God works in the lives of people through man. When you are doing good perceive it as God giving you the privilege to be an angel (God-sent) to that individual.
5. When you do good you become a channel for the receiver to obtain the blessing of God.
6. When you do good you become God's store house of His blessings. How can God's store house ever lack? Indeed, you will be blessed so you can give more.
7. When you do good the Name of the LORD is blessed and He is glorified. That is, you bring glory to God. He will also glorify His Name in your life.
8. We learn giving/doing good from the home. Parents and leaders should therefore teach children and followers the act of giving so they can practice it wherever they find themselves.
9. It is sad that some people ignore their families or close ones and rather do good to outsiders. It should start from the home.

Prayer: Heavenly Father, please help me cultivate the attitude of giving and doing good to others. For in this, I find my blessings. Amen.

What action(s) will I take today to improve my life?

_____

_____

_____

_____

June 16

Extraordinary Showers

Scripture reading: Ezekiel 34:20-27

Ezekiel 34:26
I will make them and the places all around My hill a blessing; and I will cause showers to come down in their season; there shall be showers of blessing.

1. It is the blessing of the LORD that makes us prosperous, not our works; for others toil harder than we do but gain nothing. He only blesses the works of our hands.
2. God is committed to make your life a blessing. All you have to do is to align yourself with His will and obey Him.
3. God is so committed to bless you as His son or daughter so that others will see and give glory to Him and also come to the saving knowledge of His Dear Son, Jesus Christ.
4. The blessing of God is a promise to those who obey Him and stay in His will.
5. When God blesses you, your surroundings become blessed as well. Showers of rain do not fall on just one house; it drops on multiple houses within a vicinity.
6. God wants to bless you so you can be a channel of blessing to others.
7. Irrespective of the difficult moments you may be going through God will send down His blessings on you in due season. Just continue to remain faithful to Him.
8. When your appointed season comes no one will be able to stop God's blessings from coming upon you; except you.

Prayer: Thank You LORD for the showers of blessing You bring into my life. I pray that You shall continue to keep me in Your will especially when the showers seem to delay. In Jesus' Name. Amen.

What action(s) will I take today to improve my life?

_____

_____

_____

_____

June 17

Fall in Love with the Word of God

Scripture reading: Psalm 119:97-104

Psalm 119:97
Oh, how I love Your law! It is my meditation all the day.

1. The Psalmist is filled with great joy about what the Word of God gives him and expresses it with sigh of excitement- "Oh!"
2. When you commit your life to the daily reading, listening and meditating of God's Word, He floods your heart with great joy that empowers you to accomplish great things to His glory.
3. We should cultivate the habit of loving to read and meditate on God's Word rather than out of compulsion or observing religious obligations.
4. The sweetness of the pudding is in the eating. The more you spend time with God and His Word daily and apply it to your life the more you develop love for Him. Just as it takes time and commitment to develop love for someone, so it is with the Word of God; it should be a continuous, consistent process. Like the song goes: "Falling in love with Jesus".
5. You can develop love for God's Word by spending time to meditate on it so it saturates your mind and becomes imprinted in your heart/spirit.
6. The more you meditate on God's Word while reading it, the more you would love to meditate on it throughout your day. It is just like thinking of a loved one all day long because he/she is very dear to your heart.
7. The more you meditate on God's Word the better you are able to apply it to your daily activities and gain excellent results.
8. Some Christians read the Bible hurriedly like a storybook or newspaper and still expect to understand it and benefit from it.
9. If you find it difficult to love to read God's Word, then you might not have established a personal relationship with Him (Jesus Christ). Establish a love relationship with God.

Prayer: Lovely God, Your Word is sweeter than honey. Let me develop deeper love for Your Word by spending more time with You. Thank You LORD Jesus. Amen.

What action(s) will I take today to improve my life?

_____

_____

_____

_____

June 18

Have an Open Heart to Understand the Bible

Scripture reading: John 3:1-16

John 3:4
Nicodemus said to Him, "How can a man be born when he is old? Can he enter a second time into his mother's womb and be born?"

1. Nicodemus took the literal understanding of 'being born again'. We should not just take the Word of God literally but we should focus on the spiritual meaning.
2. We should always go to God or read His Word with an open and curious mind that is eager to learn. This is one way of studying to understand God's Word- asking the Holy Spirit questions with the expectation of receiving answers.
3. Unfortunately, some people ask Christians or pastors questions just to challenge them or the Bible instead of enriching their understanding and faith. Desist from such attitude.
4. If you do not understand a portion of the Bible, it does not mean the Word is not authentic. Keep on trusting God and one day the light/truth (i.e. the true meaning) will be revealed to you.
5. The more you spend time on God's Word the clearer and deeper your understanding becomes.
6. When we are going for evangelism we should be equipped with and open our hearts to the Holy Spirit to enable us speak words that meet the specific needs and questions of people.
7. The phrase 'born-again' has become a cliché to many Christians such that we do not perceive its true meaning. We sometimes say it to inform others that we have changed but we fail to be different.
8. Even taking the phrase literally, it means that you are a new person. Biologically, how can one person be given birth to a second time? It is impossible. When a baby is born, no matter how close he/she resembles a parent, we never say that they (i.e. the baby and the parent) are the same. That is how our born-again life must be- totally different from our former ways.

Prayer: Spirit of the Living God, please give me divine understanding of Your Word. Let me live according to Your will so I can always please You. In Jesus' Name. Amen.

What action(s) will I take today to improve my life?

_____

_____

_____

_____

The way you think is the way you live. Your mind is the ruler of your life

Harry Lorayne (Secrets of Mind Power)

June 19

Sin is an Enemy

Scripture reading: Colossians 1:13-23

Colossians 1:21
And you, who once were alienated and enemies in your mind by wicked works, yet now He has reconciled.

1. Every Christian should always remember that he/she was once in the bondage of sin and eternal death.
2. A constant reminder of this fact will help us realize the need to present Christ to perishing souls and actively snatch them from Satan's bondage with passion and concern.
3. Sin is the tactic the devil uses to alienate us from God. Anytime you live in sin you become separated from God and feel isolated. Satan then is able to bring more enticing activities with the deceit of filling your void.
4. Being alienated from God is therefore a dangerous situation. It is a fearful thing to fall into the hands of the Living God (Hebrews 10:31).
5. Be very sensitive to your relationship with God in order to detect any form of alienation from God. Anytime you feel alienated from God check your relationship with Him and immediately come out from any sin that may entangles you.
6. Sin will make you become an enemy to your own mind because your conscience (i.e. in the case of the unbeliever) or the Holy Spirit (i.e. in the case of a Christian) will "wrestle" against your mind when you sin.
7. When you sin, ask for forgiveness and immediately repent. Sin becomes a bondage when you make it a behavior. It then becomes difficult to deal with it and challenging to overcome the power (spirit) behind it.
8. Constantly living by God's Word will enable you to overcome the power and influence of sin.

Prayer: Dear God. Grant me the power to overcome every influence of sin through Your Word. Thank You for reconciling me to Yourself through Jesus Christ. Amen.

What action(s) will I take today to improve my life?

_____

_____

_____

_____

June 20

The Word of God is Sure

Scripture reading: Isaiah 55:8-11

Isaiah 55:11
So shall My word be that goes forth from My mouth. It shall not return to Me void, but it shall accomplish what I please, and it shall prosper in the thing for which I sent it.

1. The Word of God is sure and definite, and will always fulfill its purpose.
2. Do not perceive God's promise as a strange or difficult thing that will struggle to come to pass. As much as we know that natural things and processes happen without coercion, so will God's Word (promise) concerning your life be if you believe in Him.
3. Naturally, you cannot take back what you say. So is God's Word. Whatever He says has no option than to come to pass because He has the power to fulfill it.
4. God's Word will never return to Him or will never rest until it accomplishes its purpose.
5. As much as the rain and snow falls on earth and do not immediately go back to the sky (through evaporation) until it causes plants to sprout, so is the Word of God.
6. Whatever we desire and pray for according to God's purpose it has no choice but to come to pass.
7. God has made us gods on earth (Psalm 82:6). So as God speaks, we should also speak to every situation.
8. Until God speaks or gives us His Word it will not be accomplished. We must cultivate the practice of speaking and prayer so that we can have whatever we desire (if it is according to His will).

Prayer: Thank You LORD for the power of Your Word. I declare that every delayed expectation in my life be fulfilled in Jesus' Name. Amen.

What action(s) will I take today to improve my life?

_____

_____

_____

_____

June 21

Leave All Behind to Encounter God

Scripture reading: John 4:7-30

John 4:28-29
The woman then left her waterpot, went her way into the city, and said to the men, "Come, see a Man who told me all things that I ever did. Could this be the Christ?"

1. You need one personal encounter with God to turn your life around. The Samaritan woman had a shocking encounter with Christ at the well that changed her life forever.
2. Humble yourself at all times for you do not know which of the interactions you have with people would be an encounter with God.
3. Always create an atmosphere of encountering God through reading and mediating on His Word, worshipping and being attentive to the Holy Spirit.
4. When you have an encounter with God He breaks all your haughtiness and defenses so you can believe and yield to His commands.
5. When you have an encounter with God He is able to reveal your past and also your future to you.
6. When you have an encounter with God put aside your sins, burdens, baggage and ambitions, and take up His purpose for your life. That will give you fulfillment, peace and success.
7. When you have an encounter with God He expects you to testify of it and share with others so they will also come to believe Him.

Prayer: Heavenly Father, teach me to humble myself to listen to Your voice. Let me always have an encounter with You in my daily activities. Amen.

What action(s) will I take today to improve my life?

_____

_____

_____

_____

June 22

Remember Your God

Scripture reading: Ecclesiastes 12:1-14

Ecclesiastes 12:1
Remember now your Creator in the days of your youth, before the difficult days come, and the years draw near when you say, "I have no pleasure in them."

1. Humans are predisposed to forget things easily unless we consciously keep reminding ourselves (probably on daily basis).
2. One usual way of forgetfulness is when things are going on well and we become comfortable. Anytime you are too comfortable check the level of your relationship with God.
3. To remember your Creator is to establish a permanent (everlasting) and consistent relationship with God.
4. It is much easier and safer to remember God in your youth because the quality of your future is highly dependent on the decisions you make in your youth. It is also because you are much prone to make mistakes during your youthful stage; but if you have God He will direct you to avoid such mistakes and enable you to make right ones.
5. "In the days of your youth"– Your relationship with God should be on daily basis because just one mistake can ruin that relationship. Also, Satan may deceive you to think you cannot re-establish the relationship. When he is successful, he can put you in bondage and you may be unable to bounce back.
6. Even if you have passed your youth and not established a relationship with God you still have the chance today (right now) to do so. It is better to modify your future than to remain in your present situation.
7. When you fail to remember God the days of trouble will surely come and you will have no ability to handle it.
8. When you stay in God, even when the days of trouble come He will grant you the capacity to overcome it.

9. The end of one who does not establish a lasting relationship with God is regretful, unfulfilling and disappointing.
10. A guarantee to remember God on daily basis is to be committed to your daily quiet-time/ morning (Bible) devotion.

Prayer: Dear God. Thank You for letting me understand that I need You for a brighter future. Please help me to acknowledge You in all my ways so I will have no regrets. In Jesus' Name. Amen.

What action(s) will I take today to improve my life?

_____

_____

_____

_____

June 23

Focus on Your Purpose

Scripture reading: Philippians 3:12-16

Philippians 3:13b-14
But one thing I do, forgetting those things which are behind and reaching forward to those things which are ahead, I press toward the goal for the prize of the upward call of God in Christ Jesus.

1. Focus on your purpose– the reason for your living.
2. You may be doing many things at a time according to the grace and strength God has given you, but you have to focus on one at a time.
3. When you focus on one thing you bring into bare all your concentration, commitment and energy toward achieving that goal. When you focus you cut off distractions.
4. Your past success can become the enemy of your future. Do not let past success keep you from pursuing the greater ones ahead.
5. Whatever you focus on eventually controls you.
6. Until you let go of your past you cannot take hold of the future. Sadly, certain situations make some people still live in their past. The easiest way to live in the past is to still hold on to sin or unforgiveness.
7. The more you write down your goals and frequently review them the better you focus on achieving them.
8. Paint a picture of the outcome of your pursuit so that it would encourage you to work towards it. Paint the picture in your mind or more effectively find one and paste it in your room (wherever you can frequently see it). If it is completion of school, paste a picture of a graduate. If it is a house you want to build, paste that dream house.
9. Achieving a goal does not happen by chance or by accident. It requires constant, persisting and committed efforts from you. It begins with a decision, followed by an action.

10. God in His infinite wisdom placed our sight (eyes) in front of our heads (not behind) so we can forget the past and focus on the future.

Prayer: My LORD and Master, I come against anything in my past that is preventing me from achieving Your purpose for my life. I receive grace and a new vision to forge on to attain the mark You have set for me. In Jesus' Name. Amen.

What action(s) will I take today to improve my life?

_____
_____
_____
_____

June 24

Make Specific Faith-based Prayers

Scripture reading: Nehemiah 6:1-9, 15

Nehemiah 6:9b
Now therefore, O God, strengthen my hands.

1. Nehemiah uses the word "now", not because it seems he is commanding God, but he is exercising (the power of) faith. Faith is NOW! (Hebrews 11:1). He needed God's intervention immediately and had to exercise faith against his enemies.

2. When the enemy is making a mockery of the power of God or making false accusations against you, you need to exercise faith for God to prove you right.

3. Prayer, engaging God into our battles, has always been and will always be the weapon of the Christian against the enemy. Until you rise up to pray God will remain dormant in your life.

4. Nehemiah said, "O God" because he was anguished and overwhelmed by the constant attempts of the enemy to halt his work- the purpose God had given him.

5. When in trouble do not lament or look for pity. Rise up to God in prayer and by faith engage Him to fight on your behalf. That is the only way Satan can back off- when you pray in faith in Jesus' Name.

6. Let your prayer be specific. God already knows the problems you are going through. Do not waste time narrating your case to Him. Go straight to the point and pray specifically for His intervention. Nehemiah prayed, "O God, strengthen my hands"

7. The devil never gives up until you finally overcome him. On your road to your journey of purpose, be prepared to fight battles through to the end.

8. Rely on the strength of God. It is the ultimate power you need to overcome the attacks of the evil one. Do not rely on your strength; it will fail you.

Prayer: Jehovah Sabaoth (The LORD of Hosts), increase my faith and fight my battles for me [name these battles]. In Jesus' Name. Amen.

What action(s) will I take today to improve my life?

_____

_____

_____

_____

June 25

Stay Glued to God in All Situations

Scripture reading: Psalm 63:1-8

Psalm 63:8
I cling to You; Your right hand upholds me.

1. To cling is to hold tightly to something; firmly attach/stick oneself to; grip or hang on to.
2. Make a decision today to always hold tightly to God no matter the hardships of life. This decision must be a daily commitment; otherwise the devil can deceive you to give up.
3. You can hold on to God through faith in Jesus Christ. Faith (in Christ) is the glue/adhesive that binds us to God.
4. We successfully exercise faith through the Word of God. How can you have faith or be grounded in faith if you do not read, listen, meditate and live by the Word of God?
5. When the storms of life are buffeting you in all directions, the only way to hang on to God is by determination through faith.
6. For the Christian another word for determination is faith. Sometimes one has a strong determination toward something, however one can later be disappointed (because we are human). When we make faith the foundation of our determination we can achieve our purpose because faith in Christ can never be moved.
7. When we hold tightly to God with determination through faith we resist any form of separation that comes our way.
8. Being firmly attached to someone is a two-way affair. God is always ready with an outstretched arm to uphold us. The onus rests on us to remain firmly connected to Him.
9. When we remain firmly attached to God no one, including Satan, can separate us from Him because His right hand upholds us.

Prayer: Thank You Heavenly Father for Your righteous right hand that upholds me. Keep me in Your presence all the time so I can fulfill Your perfect will. Amen.

What action(s) will I take today to improve my life?

_____

_____

_____

_____

*The first step towards experiencing a colorful destiny
is locating the gift of God in your life*

Bishop David Oyedepo (Exploring the Secrets of Success)

June 26

Make God Your Ultimate Source of Help

Scripture reading: Psalm 121:1-8

Psalm 121:2
My help comes from the LORD, the Maker of heaven and earth.

1. Everybody needs help in one form or the other; in one area of life or the other. The 'high and mighty' needs help. The low in social status needs help.
2. The quality of the help we obtain is a function of who gives the help or where it comes from.
3. When you ask for help you are relying on the person at least at that point in time. There is nothing wrong with that; only make sure you do not put all your trust in the person.
4. People can disappoint you, especially when you earnestly need their assistance. Make God your ultimate source of help.
5. God can be your ultimate help when you make Him your LORD; that is, make Him the owner of your life.
6. Some people seek God only when they are in need. "Do not be deceived: God cannot be mocked. A man reaps what he sows" (Galatians 6:7). Develop a consistent relationship with God by making Him your LORD and He will attend to all your needs.
7. You can totally rely on God because He is the Maker of the heavens and earth. If He created the heavens and earth what else can He not do for you? There is nothing you need that is not within the reach of heaven and earth.

Prayer: LORD, You are the hope that I cling to. I praise You for being my Help. In You, I will lack nothing good. Amen.

What action(s) will I take today to improve my life?

_____
_____
_____
_____

June 27

Make Praise a Lifestyle

Scripture reading: 1 Chronicles 16:7-14

1 Chronicles 16:8
Give praise to the LORD, proclaim His name; make known among the nations what He has done.

1. Giving praise to God should be the lifestyle of every Christian because He pours His goodness upon us all the time.
2. As much as the goodness of the LORD never ceases towards us, our praise should never stop reaching Him.
3. If you think you have nothing to praise God for, being alive alone is a great reason.
4. "Give praise to the LORD"- Giving praise to God is not an option or something you should feel like doing. It is a command. God deserves your praise.
5. When we give praise to God we show our appreciation and gratitude to Him. In so doing, we bring God to be enthroned in our praises (Psalm 22:3) and surely He will reign in our affairs.
6. When we give praise to God we are also proclaiming His name and His goodness to the nations. Giving praise is therefore a form of testimony and evangelism.
7. Satan hates and tries to discourage us from praising God because of the power in praise.
8. The praise-giver (to God) is always filled with joy, gladness of heart and great expectations for the future.

Prayer: I give praise to You LORD for who You are. Alpha and Omega, I extol Your Name for there is none like You in the heavens, on earth and beyond what man has not yet discovered. Amen.

What action(s) will I take today to improve my life?

_____
_____
_____
_____

June 28

Fully Commit Yourself to God's Work

Scripture reading: 2 Timothy 2:1-6

1 Corinthians 15:58b
Always give yourselves fully to the work of the LORD, because you know that your labor in the LORD is not in vain.

1. God has planted you on this earth to do His work, to fulfill His purpose concerning your life.
2. Success is not great wealth acquisition or being popular but it is being able to fully fulfill God's purpose for your life.
3. Being fully committed to your purpose enables you to be focused in pursuing it. The enemy will then be unsuccessful in his attempts to distract you.
4. The work of God- His purpose for your life- must be taken seriously and requires constant commitment towards its fulfillment.
5. Before you can accomplish God's purpose you must first give your life to Jesus, for He is the Author of your purpose. When you give your life to Him He makes known your purpose. This relationship with Christ also aligns you with His purpose in order to receive grace to fulfill it with no stress.
6. Do not be weary or discouraged in doing the work of God no matter how difficult it seems, because He will definitely reward you.
7. We need patience in doing God's work for if we want instant results or rewards we may give up. God has His appointed time to reward us. Wait for the LORD.

Prayer: Grant me the grace to be committed to Your purpose concerning my life. I praise You for being a faithful God and that my labor in You will never be in vain. Thank You Jesus. Amen.

What action(s) will I take today to improve my life?

_____

_____

_____

_____

June 29

There is Power in the Blood of Jesus Christ

Scripture reading: Ephesians 1:3-14

Ephesians 1:7
In Him we have redemption through His blood, the forgiveness of sins, in accordance with the riches of God's grace.

1. Satan thought he could end the ministry of Christ by killing Him. Little did he know that he was rather facilitating the redemption of man.
2. Christ was not killed- for no one can kill God- He died by his own will to fulfill His purpose.
3. The shedding of the blood of Jesus has given us redemption from the power of Satan, sin and hell.
4. It is only the blood of Jesus that has the power to forgive sin and give eternal life.
5. The only thing we need to experience the benefits of the shedding of the blood of Christ is to believe in Him. There is power in the blood of Jesus Christ.
6. When the blood of Jesus redeems you He gives you power to overcome the influence of Satan and delivers you from all His bondages.
7. The riches of the grace of God are so great to the extent of being immeasurable. He gave out His blood in this immeasurable grace. Therefore, there is nothing that God cannot do for you and through you.

Prayer: Thank You Jesus for Your redemption power that has delivered me from Satan's bondage. I pray that You shall use me to declare Your redemption to those who do not know you. Amen.

What action(s) will I take today to improve my life?

_____

_____

_____

_____

June 30

Trust in the LORD

Scripture reading: Psalm 37:1-8

Psalm 37:3
Trust in the LORD and do good; dwell in the land and enjoy safe pasture.

1. The world is suffering from one essential attribute for life, which is trust. There is a lack of trust among friends, married couples, co-workers, parents and children. Even those who do trust still have some doubts concerning the other.
2. The relentless pursuit of wealth and the creation of a niche at the expense of others have created a general sense of dishonesty, unfaithfulness and unreliability, which has subsequently led to a trust deficit in our generation. Some people just do not care about the detrimental effects of their actions on the lives of others; they only think of what they are going to achieve.
3. Despite the issue of lack of trust, we can always trust in the LORD for He is not a man to lie or one to change His mind (Numbers 23:19).
4. When evil people are using crafty means to achieve their gains, do not follow them; do not lose hope. Keep on trusting God for He makes all things beautiful in His time.
5. As you trust God, continue to do your godly duties. Do not allow yourself to be influenced by evil practices to stop your good deeds. It is your trust in God and commitment to good deeds that will create avenues to enable you reach your goals.
6. To trust the LORD is to believe in all His commands and His Word; to solely rely on Him irrespective of the difficult and evil times. It is to plunge your whole life into His hands because you believe in Him. It is to always say "Yes Sir, Master" to all He tells you because you have made Him your LORD.
7. When you trust in the LORD you are not afraid of the progress evil people make for you know their time is very short (Psalm 37:1-2). The LORD will establish your time for elevation.

8. When you trust in the LORD you will dwell in the place He leads you (no matter how bad it may be presently) for He will eventually cause you to enjoy His goodness.

Prayer: Indeed, I am blessed to have a trustworthy God. Heavenly Father, increase my faith, especially during tough moments, to trust in You. In Jesus' name. Amen.

What action(s) will I take today to improve my life?

_____

_____

_____

_____

Jesus is LORD!

You are for…
…More Signs And Wonders

Watch Out for Volume II

Printed in the United States
By Bookmasters